Library of
Davidson College

CONSCIOUS-NESS & the ULTIMATE

CONSCIOUS-NESS & the ULTIMATE

John J. Gleason, Jr.

ABINGDON
Nashville

CONSCIOUSNESS AND THE ULTIMATE

Copyright © 1981 by Abingdon

All rights reserved.
No part of this book may be reproduced in any manner whatsoever without written permission of the publisher except brief quotations embodied in critical articles or reviews. For information address Abingdon, Nashville, Tennessee.

Library of Congress Cataloging in Publication Data
GLEASON, JOHN J 1934–
 Consciousness and the ultimate.
 Includes bibliographical references.
 1. Religion. 2. Religions. 3. Psychology, Religious. 4. Jesus Christ—Person and offices.
 I. Title.
 BL48.G578   200'.1'9   80-21397

ISBN 0-687-09470-4

Scripture quotations are from the Revised Standard Version of the Bible, copyrighted 1946, 1952, © 1971, 1973 by the Division of Christian Education of the National Council of the Churches of Christ in the U.S.A. and are used by permission.

MANUFACTURED BY THE PARTHENON PRESS AT
NASHVILLE, TENNESSEE, UNITED STATES OF AMERICA

Dedicated to
My First Mother-God

CONTENTS

PREFACE... 11

PART I. HISTORY:
The Phylogeny of Consciousness of the Ultimate

1. BEGINNINGS...17
   Eliade and the History of Religions • Some Data from Archaeological Sources

2. STAGE ONE: BASIC TRUST............................... 19
   The Specific Hypothesis • Campbell and Comparative Mythology • Jung and Analytical Psychology • Bachofen and Cultural Anthropology • Cox and Sociology • Bellah and the Sociology of Religion • Noss and Comparative Religion • Summary: A Typology of the Basic Trust Stage

3. STAGE TWO: AUTONOMY............................... 29
   The Specific Hypothesis • Campbell and Comparative Mythology • Pettazoni and the Two Supreme Beings • James and the History of Religions • Cox and Sociology • Bellah and the Sociology of Religion • Noss and Comparative Religion • Summary: A Typology of the Autonomy Stage • Autonomy Illuminative Case

4. STAGE THREE: INITIATIVE............................... 38
   The Specific Hypothesis • Zoroaster—Sin and Redemption • Lao-tze—Sin and Redemption • Mahavira—Sin and Redemption • Gautama—Sin and Redemption •

Confucius—Sin and Redemption • Jesus—Sin and Redemption • Muhammad—Sin and Redemption • Summary: A Typology of the Initiative Stage

5. STAGE FOUR: INDUSTRY 47
The Specific Hypothesis • The Work of Pioneering the Kingdom of God • The Work of Materializing the Kingdom of God • The Work of Consolidating the Kingdom of God • Summary: A Typology of the Industry Stage

6. STAGE FIVE: IDENTITY 54
The Specific Hypothesis • The Coming of Age in Its Scientific Expression • The Coming of Age in Its Philosophical Expression • The Coming of Age in Its Political Expression • The Coming of Age in Its Economic Expression • The Coming of Age in Its Theological Expression • Summary: A Typology of the Identity Stage

7. STAGE SIX: INTIMACY 65
The Specific Hypothesis • Intimacy in Its Demographic Dimension • Intimacy in Its Ecological Dimension • Intimacy in Its Economic Dimension • Intimacy in Its Political Dimension • Intimacy in Its Philosophical Dimension • Intimacy in Its Sexual Dimension • Intimacy in Its Theological Dimension • Summary: A Typology of the Intimacy Stage

8. STAGE SEVEN: GENERATIVITY 77
The Specific Hypothesis • Teilhard de Chardin, Scientist/ Philosopher/ Theologian of the Creative Future • *2001: A Space Odyssey*, As a Mythic Anticipation of the Creative Future • Summary: A Typology of the Generativity Stage

9. STAGE EIGHT: INTEGRITY 86
The Specific Hypothesis • Jean-Paul Sartre, Novelist/ Playwright/Philosopher of the Destructive Future • *On the Beach*, As a Mythic Anticipation of the Destructive Future • Summary: A Typology of the Integrity Stage

PART II. PSYCHOLOGY:
The Ontogeny of Consciousness of the Ultimate

10. THE PSYCHOLOGY OF RELIGION 95
From Phylogeny to Ontogeny • Early Philosophical Threads • The New Science Versus Western Christian

Theology • The Emergence of the Psychology of Religion • The Contribution of Anton Boisen • The Crisis in the Psychology of Religion

11. THE FOUR FUNCTIONS OF THE MIND............ 103
    Beyond the Psychology of Religion • The Contribution of Carl G. Jung • The Four Functions Defined • The Four Functions Applied

12. SENSATION AND CONSCIOUSNESS OF THE ULTIMATE.. 109
    The Sensation Typology • The Sensation Type, Liturgy, and Good Works • Sensation and Natural Literalism: World A • Sensation/World A Illuminative Case

13. FEELING AND CONSCIOUSNESS OF THE ULTIMATE.. 114
    The Feeling Typology • The Feeling Type, Pastoral Care, and Glossolalia • Feeling and Conscious (Repressed) Literalism: World B • Feeling/World B Illuminative Case

14. THINKING AND CONSCIOUSNESS OF THE ULTIMATE.. 119
    The Thinking Typology • The Thinking Type and Systematic Theology • Thinking and Broken Myth: World C • Thinking/World C Illuminative Case

15. INTUITION AND CONSCIOUSNESS OF THE ULTIMATE.. 124
    The Intuition Typology • The Intuition Type and the Religious Quest • Intuition and the Monomyth: World D • Intuition/World D Illuminative Case

PART III. THEOLOGY:
A Christological Prescription for Consciousness of the Ultimate

16. A CHRISTOLOGICAL SURVEY......................... 133
    From Phylogeny to Ontogeny to Christology • Jesus Christ: Very God and Very Man (Orthodoxy) • The Christology of Divine Self-Limitation (Kenotic Theory) • The Initiator of the Kingdom of God (Liberalism; The Social Gospel) • Jesus Christ: The Lord as Servant and the Servant as Lord (Neo-orthodoxy) • Jesus Christ and the New Being (Theology of Culture) • The Incarnation in Process Theology (Process Thought) • Eschatological

Christology (Eschatological Theology) • Jesus Christ as the Self-Annihilation of God (Death-of-God Theology) • Jesus Christ as Harlequin (Theology of Juxtaposition)

17. A CHRISTOLOGICAL CRITIQUE......................142
   A Critique of Orthodoxy • A Critique of Kenotic Theory • A Critique of Liberalism • A Critique of Neo-orthodoxy • A Critique of the Theology of Culture • A Critique of Process Thought • A Critique of Eschatological Theology • A Critique of Death-of-God Theology • A Critique of the Theology of Juxtaposition

18. THE WORLD D BOON: A CHRISTOLOGICAL PRESCRIPTION...149
   A Recapitulation • A Parable • A Radical Christology • A Prescription • World D Illuminative Case: The Church of Jesus Christ the Kidnapped

19. THE PRESCRIPTION APPLIED TO WORLD C: FRAGMENTS FOR A HARLEQUINESQUE SYSTEMATIC THEOLOGY.............................. 154
   Jesus Christ as Ultimate Harlequin • God as Unity-in-Diversity-Plus • Holy Spirit as Lure to Creative Emergence • Humanity as Conscious, Creative Creature • Sin/Redemption as Movement Away From, or Toward, Unity-in-Diversity • Eschatology as Arrival at Unity-in-Diversity • World C Illuminative Case: Bokononism

20. THE PRESCRIPTION APPLIED TO WORLD B: HARLEQUINESQUE PASTORAL CARE.............165
   Introductory Comment • Harlequinesque Pastoral Care for the World A Citizen • Harlequinesque Pastoral Care for the World B Citizen • Harlequinesque Pastoral Care for the World C Citizen • Harlequinesque Pastoral Care for the World D Citizen • World B Illuminative Case: People's Temple

21. THE PRESCRIPTION APPLIED TO WORLD A: HARLEQUINESQUE MISSIONS.......................171
   Introductory Comment • In the Political Sphere • In the Demographic/Ecological/Economic Sphere • In the Scientific Sphere • In the Religious Sphere

EPILOGUE...178

NOTES.. 182

PREFACE

How did we human beings come to our present state of consciousness regarding ultimates?—that is, how did we arrive at our religious beliefs or unbelief, our religious behavior or lack of it, our religious experience or the absence thereof, and our religious knowledge (if there is such a thing)? And where do we go from here?

These are timeless, vital, and most often, inadequately answered questions. The religious impulse persists through the rise and fall of gods and god concepts; through accusations that religious expression is childish (Comte), wishful thinking (Freud), a tranquilizer used by the powerful upon the weak (Marx); through the entire history of the development of human consciousness.

Thoughtful persons have maintained in practically every historical moment that their own particular time seemed striking as a critical crossroads; yet,

> there is something in the air of the modern world: a defiance of authority, a contagious irresponsibility, a kind of moral delinquency, no longer restrained by religious or ethical faith. And these attitudes are now threatening not only personal serenity but also public order in many parts of the world.[1]

It is this "something in the air," a vague but distinctly compelling, even urgent, unease that calls forth yet another effort to ponder imponderables, to describe the ineffable, to categorize the efforts of humankind, both collectively and individually—to apprehend the ultimate. For what purpose? Enlightenment? Education? Exorcism? Yes, all these.

Any attempt to superimpose a predetermined set of categories upon the unbelievably complex ongoing experience of humankind can achieve only the most limited goals. And when such systematization involves the religious beliefs, experiences, and behavior of humankind, potential conclusions become even more ambiguous.

Assuming that an investigator—or more accurately, a theoretician—decides to press on, in spite of the tremendous odds against meaningful classification, what method should be used? Synthesis! A lifting up of discernible patterns in which the insights of several disciplines seem extremely pertinent, at the very least. Anthropology, archaeology, comparative religion, the history of religions, mythology, paleontology, philosophy, psychology, the psychology of religion, sociology, the sociology of religion, and theology—all contain materials vital to an understanding of the process of human religious development.

To make the effort is admittedly to engage in dilettantism—to sink into what Eliade calls an obsolete reductionism.[2] To resist is to fall prey to a haughty pedantry. But better a dilettante than a pedant! And even better to attempt a responsible dilettantism! Such would certainly resist the offering, willy-nilly, of yet another scheme in a field already cluttered with the rusting hulks of long-abandoned machinations, all unconvincing tries at organizing data that by definition resist empirical verification.

Such an attempt would necessarily go beyond those developmental theories equating the rise of civilization with the decline of religion; and even beyond the frequent assumption of institutional Christianity as the zenith of human religious development.

Is there any meaningful measure to be stated clearly at the outset, by which any like effort can be finally assessed? Sheldon R. Isenberg and Dennis E. Owen offer an eightfold standard to which the responsible methodology must answer, in terms of its ability to handle a complex set of interlocking problems.

First, it must bridge the gap between the sociology of religion and the psychology of religion by evaluating equally the communal religious phenomena and the religious experiences of individuals.

Second, classifications should not carry inherent value judgments, no matter how subtle, that it is better or worse to be, say, primitive or modern.

Third, the system should be comprehensive enough to allow meaningful comparisons and differentiations across geographical and time lines.

Fourth, the effort should not be reductionist, *a priori*.

Fifth, it should be able to appreciate adequately both the simple social setting of the tribe and the massive differentiation of the industrial society.

Sixth, it should be able to roll with the punches, so to speak—to absorb and recognize meanings in the inevitably present, unpredictable, and defiantly unclassifiable schisms and conversions that come.

Seventh, the theory behind the method should be able to generate empirically disconfirmable hypotheses.

Eighth, the methodology should be meaningful to, and workable for, both the personally religious and the authentically secular individual.[3]

A whopping set of standards indeed! They will be considered in the epilogue as a measure of the strengths and weaknesses of this study.

Why call such a study *Consciousness and the Ultimate*? The term consciousness is intended to apply to distinctly religious efforts, but does not exclude the unconscious religious implications of secular activity. The term ultimate replaces the word God as a less specific, and therefore more mysterious, more inclusive, catchword, even leaving room for a God beyond God.

PART I

HISTORY:
THE PHYLOGENY OF CONSCIOUSNESS OF THE ULTIMATE

CHAPTER 1

BEGINNINGS

Eliade and the History of Religions

Is meaningful data available to illuminate the very beginnings of the consciousness of ultimacy—that is, the rising religious consciousness of humanity? No. The brilliant survey and critique by Mircea Eliade regarding our capabilities to recapture what actually happened thousands upon thousands of years ago seems to have made the same sort of impact upon the history of religions that *The Quest of the Historical Jesus* of Albert Schweitzer had upon nineteenth-century historical theology. In *The Quest*, Eliade forcefully reminds us that because our oldest documents are relatively recent, in the sense that they take us no further backward into time than the Paleolithic age, we do not have the means to investigate so-called primordial religion.

Thus we can only speculate about the thought of prelithic man during many hundreds of thousands of years. From his studies Eliade concludes that because belief in "high gods" seems to have been present alongside other religious elements in the oldest cultures, we must assume that religious life has been complex from the beginning.[1]

As a historian of religions, Eliade believes that he is unable to reach the origin, the very beginning, of religion, because of the forced encounter with history. Furthermore, he sees this inability as no longer a problem for the historian of religions, though conceivably it may pose a difficulty for the philosopher or the theologian.[2] Indeed, what happened in the beginning *is* the initial problem of this study.

Some Data from Archaeological Sources

Archaeologists have found that Neanderthal man buried his dead accompanied by food and flint implements. Cro-Magnons of the Old Stone Age surrounded their dead with ornaments, as well as weapons and food; in addition, they covered the bodies with red ochre. Certain caverns contain clay figures and drawings that depict the climax of the hunt, tiny sculptured female figures with exaggerated reproductive organs and body areas associated with fertility, and vivid representations of what we today would call the medicine man.[3]

By the time of the New Stone Age, burial rites had become more complex and occasionally included human sacrifice. There were cremations, as well as interment under large boulders, in specially built caves, and in stone chambers. Carefully constructed monuments and alignments such as Stonehenge seem to have been connected with religious observance, as were relics symbolizing sun, moon, stars, and trees.[4]

During the transition from hunting to agriculture and a more settled village life, there can be seen an increasingly verifiable association of woman with the earth and its life-giving and sustaining capabilities. Great numbers of the female figurines, probably used in religious rites to assure fertility and rich harvests, date from this period.[5]

CHAPTER 2

STAGE ONE: BASIC TRUST

The Specific Hypothesis

In the Near East, about 5000 B.C., a basic trust stage in the development of religious consciousness began to come into focus. It is illustrated by the mother, or mother figure, who responds, with varying degrees of success, to the expressed needs of the child during the first year of life: the need for milk and gradually for more solid fare, with the related oral pleasures; the need for warmth, for dryness, for general body comforts; the need for loving attention; the need for play; the need for laughter; the need for an underlying sense of worth, satisfaction, well-being.

Erik H. Erikson contends that in this first year of life every child experiences a developmental crisis in which he or she either learns basic trust or, to varying degrees, fails—that is, learns mistrust. At approximately this same developmental moment the mother figure is, in a practical, phenomenological sense, the child's first god; thus every child learns the first feeling-level, unconscious lessons about the nature and attributes of as yet indistinguishable gods/God by the way the mother figure meets or fails to meet its needs.[1]

Campbell and Comparative Mythology

Compare the following analysis by Joseph Campbell of the presence of and uses for the many female figurines, with the preceding hypothesis, especially concerning the child's first-year feeling-level religious lessons about gods, learned at the mother's breast.

Campbell maintains that the existence of so many female figurines from the period suggests an obvious analogy between woman's life-giving and nourishing powers and similar powers in the earth: Stone Age humanity associated fertile womanhood with the motherhood of nature. Campbell goes on to accuse archaeologists of pretending ignorance as to what services the numerous female figurines might have rendered to the households for which they were designed, on the grounds that there is no writing from this preliterate age and no knowledge, therefore, of its myths and rites.

Campbell states that our knowledge of such services, from the immediately succeeding period to present day, is sufficient to assume similar Neolithic functions: to give magical aid to women in conception and childbirth: to stand in house shrines, protecting the occupants from spiritual and physical danger and receiving daily prayers; to serve as the focus for meditation upon the deeper questions of being; to provide protection to crops, cattle, children, and even sailors and merchants.[2]

Care-giving Mother-God characterizes each human being's source of help in the first year of life as well as the focal point of Neolithic man's religious devotion. Campbell speaks of certain imprints upon the nervous system as being the source of some of the most familiar myth-images. In a fascinating discourse on myths having their bases within the blissful state of the child at its mother's breast or within that condition's horrible opposite, he weaves into the narrative accounts of witches, princesses, ogresses, goddesses, and prototypes of the Madonna of the Middle Ages in mythology and art. He summarizes,

> And so, in mythology and rite, as well as in the psychology of the infant, we find the imagery of the mother associated almost equally with beatitude and danger, birth and death, the inexhaustible nourishing breast and the tearing claws of the ogress. The heavenly realm, where the paradisial meal is served forever, and Olympus, the mountain of the gods, where ambrosia flows—these, certainly, are but versions fit for saints and heroes of

STAGE ONE: BASIC TRUST

the bliss of the well-nursed child. And the primary imprint of which the fury and fright of the disemboweling maw of hell is the adult amplification, is no less certainly the child's own fantasies of its raging body—its whole universe—torn apart.[3]

Campbell's description of the dichotomy in mythology between bliss and horror, between trust-inducing and mistrust-producing experiences, bears a startling resemblance to Erikson's first-year-of-life psychological crisis—basic trust versus mistrust—with the overlay that at this stage, basic feeling-level lessons are being learned about the nature of gods, god, God, from the way the mother responds to the needs of the child.

Jung and Analytical Psychology

In his analytical psychology, C. G. Jung hypothesized that beneath that more or less superficial layer of the unconscious, which he termed the personal unconscious, is a deeper layer called the collective unconscious. Whereas the personal unconscious is individual in that it derives from acquired personal experience, the collective unconscious "has contents and modes of behavior that are more or less the same everywhere and in all individuals" and are therefore universal.[4] Whereas the contents of the personal unconscious primarily comprise feeling-toned complexes—that is, the personal and private aspect of psychic life—the collective unconscious contains what Jung calls archetypes.

By archetypes, Jung means a hypothetical and even irrepresentable model, in the same sense that the pattern of behavior in biology is not representable. The archetype "is essentially an unconscious content that is altered by becoming conscious and by being perceived, and it takes its color from the individual consciousness in which it happens to appear."[5] Well-known expressions of the archetypes, according to Jung, are tribal lore, myth, and fairy tale.

In fact, he sees all the mythologized processes of nature—summer and winter, phases of the moon, rainy seasons, and so on—as symbolic expressions of that unconscious inner drama of the psyche which become accessible to human consciousness by projective mirroring in natural events.

Pertinent to this discussion is Jung's description of the mother archetype. He acknowledges that the concept of the Great Mother belongs to the field of comparative religion, but holds that as a symbol, it is a derivative of the mother archetype.[6]

Representing the good-mother-god-of-basic-trust, Jung cites the many examples of the mother archetype in mythology: the mother who reappears as the maiden in the myth of Demeter and Kore; the mother who is also the beloved, as in the Cybele-Attis myth. He sees more figurative symbols of the mother in images representing the goal of human longing for redemption: paradise, the kingdom of God, and the heavenly Jerusalem. According to Jung, many objects inspiring devotion and awe, such as church, university, nation, heaven, earth, the sea, underworld, moon, and even matter itself, can be mother symbols, along with those that represent fertility and fruitfulness—a garden, the cornucopia, a plowed field.[7]

To symbolize the bad-mother-god-of-mistrust, he mentions the goddess of fate, and evil symbols such as the witch, any devouring animal, the grave, deep water, and death. Jung holds that, significant as the mother is, "all those influences which the literature describes as being exerted on the children do not come from the mother herself, but rather from the archetype projected upon her, which gives her a mythological background and invests her with authority and numinosity."[8]

Bachofen and Cultural Anthropology

J. J. Bachofen, in his 1861 work, *Das Mutterrecht*, argued that human society began in a state of primitive promiscuity, in which there was no regulation of behavior; no social organization whatever. A second stage of cultural evolution, according to Bachofen, was associated with woman's invention of agriculture.

Here Bachofen saw women ruling the household and the

STAGE ONE: BASIC TRUST

state, and passing their property and their names to their children. A set of religious beliefs centering upon an earth goddess was an essential ingredient in his matrilineal stage. A cult grew up about this earth goddess and, dependent upon the religious mentality of women, gave rise to the political structure and descent rule, and only late in cultural evolution did it give way to a patrilineal and patriarchal system.[9]

Bachofen and other nineteenth-century matriarchal theorists soon fell out of favor in the onrush of empirically based field-work techniques, the confusion over definitions of terms, and the discarding of all theories of general development, and effort became concentrated upon the functional approach to the study of institutions in a society.[10]

A trend toward renewal of the work begun by Bachofen to hammer out a typology of general levels of cultural development is acknowledged openly in the proceedings of the Social Science Research Council's summer seminar at Harvard in 1954. Although, in the conclusions drawn from the masses of data generated by the seminar, the researchers resist equating the rise of matriliny with the rise of horticulture and therefore refuse to call this set of factors a stage in general evolution, "where results are significant, matrilineal systems are relatively commoner in 'dominant horticulture' than in any other category, by comparison with patrilineals or bilaterals."[11]

At least some cultural anthropologists, rightfully having purged their discipline of the sweeping generalities of their pioneering predecessors, are returning ever so gingerly to an acknowledgment of some sort of ascendency by women as a correlate of the establishment of agriculture. Such a move seems an affirmation, though vague, of the hypothesis elucidated in this study about an initial basic trust stage in the developing religious consciousness of humankind, with distinct features analogous to those seen within the mother-child relationship of individuals.

Cox and Sociology

The basic trust stage of developing religious consciousness is further characterized by the groupings of persons in tribal societies. For Harvey Cox, tribal society is a stage in human social development variously described as totemic, primitive, preliterate, prelogical, and even savage. He sees the variety of terms as illustrative of the problem. They include the descriptive and the pejorative, as well as those designed to point up various aspects in the lives of peoples extremely remote from Cox's technopolis.[12]

But Cox goes on to offer some typological statements. The tribe was a "family writ large," with roots in a common mythological past and members "locked together in lines of consanguinity," giving an unquestioned place and a secure identity to each person by providing answers, through tribal tradition, to the great questions of human existence. Dance, chant, carved figurine, and mask—the total ritual provided an "utterly complete catalog of images, identities and values" and communicated the "oughts" regarding marriage, vocation, and purpose of life.

Tribal man is hardly a personal "self" in our modern sense of the word. He does not so much live in a tribe; the tribe lives in him. He is the tribe's subjective expression. He grasps himself within a closed system of compact meanings in which there is no room for any transcendent point of view or critical detachment. Man and nature, the animals and the gods, all form one continuous life process whose meaning courses through it just below the surface and can erupt anywhere in a transparent moment of magical or religious power.[13]

This diffusion of identity, this symbiotic relationship between tribal member and tribe itself, seems strikingly analogous to that relationship of merged egos between the mother and her newly born child, so often observed and described in individual developmental literature, in which basic trust is being experienced and corporate lessons about the nature of gods, god, God, are being learned at the feeling level.

Bellah and the Sociology of Religion

Robert N. Bellah has hypothesized five stages in the religious evolution of humankind.[14] In that scheme he attempts to identify each stage by describing its symbol

STAGE ONE: BASIC TRUST

system, religious actions, social organization, and implications for social action in general.

The basic trust stage described here occurs somewhere between Bellah's first stage, "primitive," and his second, "archaic," with some characteristics of both. He uses the primitive concept in a very restricted sense, describing the predominantly prelithic Australian culture-area phenomena almost exclusively. This culture's symbol-system centers upon the Australian words translated as "the dreaming"—a "time out of time," an "everywhen"—inhabited by ancestral figures, some human, some animal. Its two main features are "the very high degree to which the mythical world is related to the detailed features of the actual world" and the fluidity and free-associational nature of its organization.[15]

Bellah characterizes primitive religious action not by worship or by sacrifice, but by identification, participation, acting out—a ritual par excellence—in which the slight distance that exists between man and mythical beings disappears. In this primitive stage, religious organization as a separate social structure simply does not exist. The social implications of ritual life are to reinforce societal solidarity, "to induct the young into the norms of tribal behavior," to affirm life as a "one possibility thing."[16]

In the archaic symbol-system, on the other hand, the mythical beings "are more objectified, conceived as actively and sometimes willfully controlling the natural and human world, and as beings with whom men must deal in a definite and purposive way; in a word they have become gods." Furthermore, archaic religious action centers on communication between the more objectified gods and their human subjects via cultic worship and sacrifice. Here religious organization remains merged with other social structures, though the emergence of a two-class system (workers and leaders) has its religious implications. The upper-class group assumes superior religious status as well as military and political power. Archaic social implications are similar to those in the primitive stage, in that "traditional social structures and social practices are considered to be grounded in the divinely instituted cosmic order, and there is little tension between religious demand and social conformity."[17]

One more vote seems cast here by Bellah for the recognition of an early period involving the symbiotic intertwining of tribe, tribal members, and their gods—a corporate, merged identity out of which only gradually began to emerge the distinctions between gods and humans, workers and leaders, priests and laity, tribe and individuals.

Noss and Comparative Religion

John B. Noss lists what he calls characteristic features of religion in primitive cultures. Though the concept of a so-called primitive mind-set or mentality has been challenged by Eliade and others, Noss's list is summarized here to add some of the possible ingredients of the basic trust stage. The list includes awe for the sacred (that which signifies supernatural potency), expression of anxiety in ritual, rituals of expectancy, interweaving of myth and ritual, bipolarity of religion and magic (the effort to control the powers of the world through fetishism, shamanism, and/or popular magic), prayer, divination, belief in mana (occult force or indwelling power), animism (belief that motionless objects as well as moving creatures possess spirits), veneration and worship of spirits, recognition of high gods, tabu (a person or thing so highly charged with power that even to touch it is highly dangerous), purification rites, sacrifice (the giving up of something to the gods), certain attitudes toward the dead (including worship), and totemism (a sense of intimate relationship with other orders of life and even with inanimate objects).[18]

Summary: A Typology of the Basic Trust Stage

During the period of transition from a hunting to an agricultural economy, in the Near East a time centering on the year 5000 B.C., an increasingly distinct stage in the development of human religious consciousness becomes discernible. Its features include a growing appreciation of the life-giving

STAGE ONE: BASIC TRUST

and nourishing powers of woman as analogous to those of the earth, and thereby to the motherhood of nature; the extensive use of the tiny sculptured female figurines associated with fertility; a growing number of mythological figures representing both the inexhaustible nourishing breast of the good mother and the tearing claws of the ogress; a Great Mother archetype formation in the layer of the human psyche beneath the personal unconscious, at the level of the collective unconscious; the establishment of a matriarchal cluster involving matriliny and the beginnings of earth goddess worship; the grouping of families into tribal social organization, in which tribe, tribal members, symbol system, religious and social actions—all affirm life as a one-possibility thing in the sense of Erikson's term, basic trust. These are at least some of the qualities attributed by comparative religion to the so-called primitive mind and its religious expression—a symbiotic merging of identities analogous to the ego states of a mother and her newborn child, in which feeling-level lessons are learned by the tribe/tribal members about gods, god, God, as being basically either trustworthy or not trustworthy.

No evidence is available to demonstrate the existence of a tribe in the Near East at about 5000 B.C. with *all* the features of the basic trust stage typology; it is, after all, only a typology. However, Heinrich Zimmer's commentary on a Hindu version of the story of the Great Goddess is illuminative.

If one inquires to know her ultimate origin, the oldest textual remains and images can carry us back only so far, and permit us to say: "Thus she appeared in those early times; so-and-so she may have been named; and in such-and-such a manner she seems to have been revered." But with that we have come to the end of what can be said; with that we have come to the primitive problem of her comprehension and being. She is the *primum mobile*, the first beginning, the material matrix out of which all comes forth. To question beyond her into her antecedents and origin, is not to understand her, is indeed to misunderstand and underestimate, in fact to insult her. And anyone attempting such a thing well might suffer the calamity that befell that smart young adept who undertook to unveil the veiled image of the Goddess in the ancient Eyptian temple of Sais, and whose tongue was paralysed forever by the shock of what he saw. According to the Greek tradition the

CONSCIOUSNESS AND THE ULTIMATE

Goddess has declared of herself: "no one has lifted my veil." It is a question not exactly of the veil, but of the garment that covers her female nakedness—the veil is a later misinterpretation for the sake of decency. The meaning is: I am the Mother without a spouse, the Original Mother; all are my children, and therefore none has ever dared to approach me; the impudent one who should attempt it shames the Mother; and that is the reason for the curse.[19]

CHAPTER 3

STAGE TWO: AUTONOMY

The Specific Hypothesis

With the amalgamation of tribes into city-kingdoms; the refinement of grain agriculture and stockbreeding; the invasions of nomadic peoples; the development of writing and of the wheel; the appearance of currency, mathematics, the calendar, kingship, and priestcraft; and the emergence of the national, transcending tribal belief (all with special attention to the Near East), a second stage, autonomy, can be perceived in the developing religious consciousness.

A second stage in the development of individuals takes place in the second, third, and fourth years of life and becomes dramatized in Western culture by toilet training. Whereas the basic trust stage in individual development focuses on oral needs, the autonomy stage is represented by the struggle between the child and the parents for control over the eliminative body functions—that is, anal needs. The child seeks autonomy as a power within himself and says in essence, "I'll let go when and where I want, with what I want." The parents counter with, "You should hold on except under certain conditions, which we specify."

If the parents are sensitive, lovingly but firmly inviting the child to take more and more responsibility in this area, an increasing sense of autonomy, of selfhood, of well-being about the goodness of self and the products of self results. If the parents harshly, condemningly, and rigidly enforce the law and thereby convey to the child a sense that he and/or the products of his body are evil, then the child comes through this psychosocial crisis filled with doubts about himself, his worth, and the worth of products of his body and mind.

During this whole process, feeling-level theological lessons are being learned regarding good versus evil, law and order, and so forth, which will determine the way a person looks at self, others, the world, and God. A fundamentalist mind-set easily divides all into neat either/or categories of white or black, right or wrong, heaven or hell, good or evil, while the ideal child develops a sense of his own autonomy and worth and is able to see self, others, the world, and God in their polarities, their conflicts, and at times, their subtle shades of gray.[1]

This individual struggle for autonomy, in which feeling-level lessons about what is good and what is evil are being learned, appears to have been acted out on a grand scale during this historical period, as tribal entities began the outward push for greater territories and power, with the attending belief system: We are good; They are evil and should be enslaved or destroyed. A further focusing of the drama, with great religious implications, involved the clash between the nomadic herdsmen and the farming village-dwellers—the thrusts of the sky god worshipers into the lands of the earth mother goddess.

Campbell and Comparative Mythology

Joseph Campbell sees the widespread influence, the peace, and the bounty of the goddess described in chapter 2 as reaching the wild nomadic herders of cattle, sheep, and goats in two matrices: the Syro-Arabian desert and the great grasslands of central Europe. Campbell's studies lead him to conclude that by 3500 B.C., these nomads, with their more masculine, aggressive life-style and their accompanying more masculine, aggressive god-myths, were descending upon the farming villages and towns to plunder and ravage and, even more severely, remaining to maintain control and enslave the farming people.[2]

By 3000 B.C. the invaders had established power states; by 1500 B.C., strong men, including Sargon of Agade (c. 2350 B.C.)

STAGE TWO: AUTONOMY

and Hammurabi of Babylon (c. 1728–1686 B.C.), had developed a new and distinct relationship to the goddess. To illustrate, Campbell quotes one of the chronicles of Sargon, which tells of a mother of lowly station, an unknown father, a secretive birth, transport by his mother's effort in a basket of rushes down the river, and discovery and nurture by an irrigator who raised him as a gardener—a lover of the goddess.

This is an example of the myth of the birth of the hero, extant in over seventy variants in literature, including the biblical account of Moses' life, in which the older formula of the goddess and her son is altered to transfer the emphasis to the son himself, now neither god nor sacrifice, but a strong male with political ambitions.[3]

The next step was to project this royal inflation back upon the king of gods, a model of, and for, the emerging earthly Oriental-despot kingship, clearly illustrated in the prelude to the Law of Hammurabi. There Hammurabi responds to a specific call from the gods to wipe out the wicked and evil, to bring about the reign of goodness and righteousness, and to go forth like the sun, to illuminate the land.[4]

Campbell cites the victory of Marduk, patron god of the city of Babylon, over his great-great-great-grandmother Tiamat, as the best-known mythic example of the ascendancy of male over female, sky over earth, sun god over goddess. This Babylonian epic of creation was preserved for us in the library of King Ashurbanipal of Assyria, who lived a full millennium later (c. 668–630 B.C.).[5]

The struggle for autonomy among tribes—between nomadic herdsmen and farming villagers, between the sky gods and the earth goddesses—is a sweeping and grim analogy to the struggle for autonomy in individual development, in which the conflict between the good tribe (us) versus the evil tribe (them) was settled inexorably, irrevocably, and violently with the spear, the hand ax, and the spilling of blood by victorious warrior kings.

Pettazoni and the Two Supreme Beings

Raffaele Pettazoni adds his voice, in a more theoretical sense, to that of Joseph Campbell when he states that there is a phenomenology of a supreme being oriented toward the earth and a phenomenology of a supreme being oriented toward the sky. Although he does not risk any suggestion of sequentiality and speaks of the two phenomenologies as a polarity, Pettazoni sees both as legitimate, because each is a manifestation of the divine. Furthermore, they spring forth out of existential anxieties, not out of intellectual requirements.

He recognizes that behind Mother Earth there stands a long tradition of matriarchal agricultural civilization and that behind Heavenly Father there exists a long tradition of patriarchal pastoral civilization. His central idea is that in either case, there are reasons vital to human existence in the notion of a supreme being.

Granted, the sky extends equally over farmer and nomadic herdsman, but the farmer's sacred experience of the sky, as basically generated from the earth, is quite different from that of the herdsman, for whom the sky is a diffuse presence that intrudes on humans constantly everywhere, as an all-seeing eye. Conversely, the earth on which both farmer and herdsman stand is experienced by the farmer as mother, nurturer, giver of fruits and flowers for sustenance and joy; in sharp contrast is the herdsman's experience of the earth as a sterile, boundless extension of steppe.[6]

James and the History of Religions

E. O. James, professor emeritus of the history and philosophy of religion at the University of London, in the 1962 Jordan Lectures in Comparative Religion, stated his conclusion that from a more basic goddess cult going back to the upper Paleolithic age, there emerged, especially in arid regions where water was an urgent need, the figure of the sky god. In nearly every ancient pantheon from the Neolithic period onward, James found such a god, whose primary concerns were the weather, the atmosphere, and the creative process in general, occasionally obscured, however, by a drift either toward solarization (e.g., Ikhnaton and his sun god, Aton, in Egypt) or toward absolute transcendence (e.g., the relatively recent God of Deism).[7]

From the evidence, James strongly resists the once popular notion of an orderly progression from animism to polytheism to monotheism, and also the idea of the sky gods, or "high gods," as indicative of a sort of primeval monotheism. Though assigned a value greater than that of other supernatural beings (yet most often without a cultus and ritualized accessibility), sky gods existed in relationship to the lesser gods and their delegated functions in what James calls a monolatry. To document his case, James cites many examples of sky gods, including Yahweh.[8]

Cox and Sociology

Harvey Cox sees this period as a shattering step from tribe to town, when the appearance of currency and writing, especially, enormously expanded the possible occasions for human interaction and served to free persons from tradition-dictated relationships. Cox offers the illustration of a man with a sheep who wishes to barter for bread. He must find a person who has both bread and a wish for wool or lamb stew. Since in a barter society, the roles of sheep-raiser and bread-baker were usually passed from father to son within the tribe, the range of possibilities was limited to that directed by tradition. Give that same sheep-raiser a market and the jingle of coins, and a whole new world opens up to him—the world of the town![9]

Similarly, writing undercut dependence upon the shaman or oracle, as individuals gained direct access to parchments—to knowledge and its accompanying power. Now a stranger with knowledge could, with luck, gain access to a town culture and citizenship, whereas formerly, access to a tribe had been solely an accident of birth.

In the movement from tribe to town to city, Cox sees as symbolic tragic figures, Antigone, who represents the transition from kinship to civic loyalties, and Socrates, who refused to accept the gods of the city as being unqualifiedly important and left the door open for a higher, more universal order—the community of humankind.[10]

CONSCIOUSNESS AND THE ULTIMATE

Bellah and the Sociology of Religion

In Bellah's scheme, this phase in the developing religious consciousness of humankind is more fully equatable with his archaic stage, in which mythical beings are much more definitely characterized in a religious symbol-system. Archaic religious action takes the form of a cult in which the distinction between persons as subjects, and gods as objects, is much more clear. Religious organization increases, with the increasing complexity of social structures, toward a multiplication of cults. The struggle between rival groups is seen as a struggle between rival deities, or even as a deity's change of favor from one group to another. The rise of such farsighted figures as Socrates signals the advent of yet the next stage of Bellah's outline, "historic," in the sense of movement toward confrontations, implying that political acts could be judged in terms of standards not ultimately controllable by political authorities.[11]

Noss and Comparative Religion

In his chapter on national religions of the past in *Man's Religions,* John B. Noss sketches out the parallel consolidation processes of both tribe-to-kingdom and local-god-to-divine amalgamation. He cites the development of the Sumero-Akkadian pantheon as one of many examples of this side-by-side rise of nations and prominent gods. Of the total of nearly two thousand gods, representing every aspect of nature, six deities emerged as the most powerful. Interestingly, each of the six was the deity of a great city: Anu, the sky god, was from the city of Uruk; Enlil, the air god, from Nippur; Nanna, the moon god, from Ur; Utu, later called Shamash, was the sun god from Larsa; Enki, the water god, resided at Eridu; and Ninhursag, the mother goddess, ruled at Kish. An even further consolidation into triads of Anu-Enlil-Ea and Shamash-Sin-Ishtar took place (Enki had become Ea, Nanna was now Sin, and Ninhursag was identified as Ishtar).

Then with the rise of Babylon, its once obscure god Marduk ascended into prominence, finally all but absorbing

STAGE TWO: AUTONOMY

the surrounding gods. Ea became Marduk's father, and thus Marduk absorbed the wisdom of Ea; he even took credit for Enlil's victory over Tiamat, the dragon of chaos, as he took on Enlil's chief attributes. Noss sees similar consolidations of power and gods as having occurred in Egypt, Greece, Rome, and northern Europe.[12]

Summary: A Typology of the Autonomy Stage

A second stage, autonomy, can be perceived in the developing religious consciousness of humankind (with special attention to the Near East). This second stage, roughly analogous to Erikson's second stage of individual psychosocial development, is discernible by the presence of several factors. These factors include the amalgamation of tribes into city-kingdoms, with the accompanying amalgamation of tribal gods into hyphened-multiple-name gods; the development of myths of the birth of the hero, in which warrior kings become the central figures and earth goddesses become their consorts; a distinction in perspective toward earth and sky, farmer and herdsman; the opening up of geometrically increasing possibilities for human interaction in the movement from tribe to town with the advent of writing, the wheel, currency as a medium of exchange, the calendar, the refinement of agriculture and stockbreeding, kingship, priestcraft, and the emergence of the national idea as transcending tribal belief; the firming up of religious rite and cult, the increasing objectification of gods, and the resulting struggle between deities who were good or evil, depending on which group was describing the good and the evil; the ascendancy of sky gods to prominence over earth goddesses within the emerging pantheons and their delegation of specific functions to the lesser gods, as the sky gods became increasingly remote and inaccessible.

Autonomy Illuminative Case

A historical example of the processes at work within the autonomy stage in humankind's rising consciousness of the ultimate is the case of the formative years in the national life of Israel. This study assumes, with the majority of competent authorities, that there was an enslavement in Egypt of some of the Hebrew tribes, an escape, a return to the desert at about 1250 B.C., and a formation under Moses' leadership of a theocratic confederacy, which was the nucleus for the mono-Yahwist development of Israel.[13]

The Genesis narratives reveal that worship of *elim* at local sanctuaries in Palestine was practiced by the patriarchs in a fashion indistinguishable from other rituals of the period throughout Asia Minor.[14] W. F. Albright, citing Alt, affirms that those divine appellations formed with the prefix "El" (Genesis 14–35) are mentioned generally in connection with very early shrines and therefore are definitely pre-Israelite. He found, further, at Jericho, an archaeologically illustrated pantheon triad, with a father god, El, a mother goddess (possibly Anath), and a son who appears as the storm god (probably Shaddai).[15] El Elyon (God Most High—Gen. 14:18), El Roi (God of a Vision—Gen. 16:13), El Shaddai (God Almighty—Gen. 17:1), and El Olan (the Everlasting God—Gen. 21:33) are examples of the El-prefix gods of Palestine before the time of Moses.

If Yahweh is not mentioned in scholarly surveys of the gods of pre-Mosaic Palestine, from whence did Yahweh come? C. S. Rankin, writing in the section "Names of Gods" in *A Theological Word Book of the Bible,* holds that Jahweh, the special name of the God of Israel, appears from the descriptions given him to have been "a sky-God, a God of thunder and lightning (Exod. 19:16, 20:18; I Kings 18:38). Thunder is his voice (Exod. 19:19; Job 37:5; Amos 1:2), lightning flashes are his arrows (Ps. 18:14; Hab. 3:11)."[16] Rankin goes on to suggest possible origins for Yahweh in the Kenite or Midianite traditions, since Moses' father-in-law was a Kenite (Judg. 1:16) or a Midianite (Exod. 3:1).

With the consolidation of power in the Hebrew tribal confederacy, a title strongly suggesting a parallel consolidation of god-power emerged: Jahweh Zeba'oth, God of Hosts. Holscher and Eichrodt see the term hosts as a reference to hosts of spirits, demons, and elohim in general (e.g., Gen. 32:1-2). In a later stage, Yahweh Zeba'oth

STAGE TWO: AUTONOMY

probably referred to the God of the armies of Israel or to the stars, after the original significance had been lost.[17]

As Israel moved from tribal confederacy and polytheistic thought into a monotheistic national identity, the ultimate compliment was paid to Yahweh Zeba'oth as having achieved supremacy over all the other gods: There was no further need to speak his name! In fact the stage was reached in the late Hellenistic period when even the use of the tetragram JHWH was forbidden as an irreverent act.[18]

CHAPTER 4

STAGE THREE: INITIATIVE

The Specific Hypothesis

In an epigenetic pleroma centering upon the period 660 B.C. (one estimated birth date for Zoroaster) through A.D. 632 (the death of Muhammad), the seven men who founded lasting world religions were born, lived their lives, did their work, and died. The men, their dates, and the religion each established are: Zoroaster (660 B.C.– ?), Zoroastrianism; Lao-tze (604–531 B.C.), Taoism; Mahavira (599–527 B.C.), Jainism; Gautama (563–480 B.C.), Buddhism; Confucius (551–479 B.C.), Confucianism; Jesus (9 B.C.–A.D. 24), Christianity; Muhammad (A.D. 571–632), Islam.[1]

This ground swell—this rising up of individual religious genius all around the world at a particular historical moment—signals the arrival of a third stage in the religious development of humankind, the initiative stage, roughly analogous to Erikson's third stage.

In individual development, this third stage, occurring about age four through six, involves the taking of initiative by the child in reaching out to his or her world in general and to the parent of the opposite sex in particular, in a vague but nevertheless sexual attraction. In the playing out of this drama within the family context, it is hoped that the child experiences the forgiveness and redemption offered by the parent of the same sex, while simultaneously bumping into the limit set by both parents: One cannot commit the sin of having the parent of the opposite sex all to oneself.[2]

STAGE THREE: INITIATIVE

On a grand historical scale, it is the personally founded world religions that internalize the battle between good and evil within the human psyche and thereby refine the doctrines of sin and redemption.

Zoroaster—Sin and Redemption

Zoroaster, or Zarathushtra, probably the earliest of these seven religion founders, was born in Media, or Bactria, to a landed proprietor and his wife. At twenty, he left his parents and the wife they had chosen for him, taking the initiative (in the Eriksonian sense of the word) to seek answers to his religious questions. At age thirty he received a revelation in which he came into the presence of the supreme being, Ahura Mazda, who instructed him in the matters of the true religion.[3]

Although the words sin, salvation, and redemption are not a part of the vocabulary of Zoroaster or of the Zoroastrian scriptures,[4] he poses the equivalent of the What must I do to be saved? question as recorded in the *Gathas*, or *Hymns:* "How shall we rid ourselves of evil?" During his remaining life and ministry, Zoroaster acted out Ahura Mazda's response to that question, establishing a belief system that holds each person's soul to be the scene of a war between good and evil.

In the light of this study, Zoroaster, the earliest of the religion founders, stands as a truly transitional figure between stages two and three, formalizing at the core of his religious system the struggle between good and evil, described as gradually crystallizing in stage two; and offering at the outset of stage three a fresh alternative to the old external way of coping with evil via the conquest and slaughter of rival tribes—namely, by internalizing the battle and by showing persons how to make right choices (redemption) as a way of conquering evil (sin). In the sense that these individual right choices, according to Zoroaster, involved repudiating the traditional religion (parent?) of the day, his initiative led the people to a literal killing of that parent religion in a symbolic, vaguely Oedipal way not unlike the vague, painful struggle within individuals age four through six.

Lao-tze—Sin and Redemption

According to tradition (so blurred that some scholars even doubt his historicity), Lao-tze, or Lao Tan, was born in the state of Ch'u. He began to question the wisdom of having any government at all (a symbolic killing of the father?) while serving as curator of the imperial archives. Concluding that his high position was a vain and false one, he resigned and, driven by a desire to move into the unknown (an expression of Eriksonian initiative?), fled from the society he had decided was corrupt. On his way out the westernmost gate, the gatekeeper persuaded him to pause long enough to set forth his beliefs. He did so in what is now known as the *Tao Te Ching*.[5]

As in Zoroastrianism, the concepts of sin, salvation, and redemption do not appear, as such, in Taoism. However, the most commonly accepted English translation of Tao, "The Way," strongly suggests a direction away from sin and toward, if not specifically salvation/redemption, at least a greater harmony with the created order, through the application of a mystical, hard-to-define wisdom, involving greater appreciation of, and flowing along with, the natural rhythms of birth-life-death-rebirth. Thus sin could be equatable with insensitivity to, and disharmony with, such rhythms. Who is the perfect man of Tao?

He is cautious, like one who crosses a stream in winter;
He is hesitating, like one who fears his neighbors;
He is modest, like one who is a guest;
He is yielding, like ice that is going to melt;
He is simple, like wood that is not yet wrought;
He is vacant, like valleys that are hollow;
He is dim, like water that is turbid;
For who is able to purify the dark till it becomes slowly light?
Who is able to calm the turbid till it slowly clears?
Who is able to quicken the stagnant till it slowly makes progress?
He who follows these principles does not desire fullness.
Because he is not full, therefore when he becomes decayed he can renew.[6]

STAGE THREE: INITIATIVE

Mahavira—Sin and Redemption

In contrast to Zoroaster and Lao-tze, Mahavira (which translates as "hero" or "great man"), originally known as Nataputta Vardhamana, was born to a rajah near Vaisali, in India, and grew up in luxury. At the age of thirty, he spoke specifically of sin and redemption, after he had renounced his wife, daughter, and princely surroundings to enter a life of severe asceticism. Again in an Oedipal rejection of father, father's way of life, and father's religion (Hinduism), a religious figure is seen to take the initiative (Erikson) as Mahavira thrust his way into an ascetic order; and a short time later, he thrust even beyond that order and shed his clothes, embarking upon a life of naked wanderings for twelve years, seeking moksha (deliverance from the sins of killing living things, lying speech, greed, sexual pleasure, and attachments of any kind). In the thirteenth year, Mahavira achieved the salvation of his soul: He reached Nirvana in a complete victory over the body and the desires that bind to this world of sinful matter. After thirty years of teaching, he died and now enjoys total bliss in a place of reward no longer subject to rebirth. (The Hindu belief in Nirvana was never seriously questioned by Mahavira or by his followers, the Jains.) An angry repudiation of the Hindu priestly caste, Mahavira's way of salvation is completely self-attained by the practice of austerities; the elaborate prayers and sacrifices of the Brahmins are useless. Furthermore, in a God-is-dead fashion, Mahavira declared that there is no Brahmin-Atman holding the universe together as the Hindu priests had described. The total focus is upon liberation of the precious eternal individual soul from the evil that encompasses it, using the methods of Mahavira.[7]

Gautama—Sin and Redemption

Siddhartha Gautama, founder of Buddhism, was born in fertile northern India, the son of a petty chief of the Sakya clan. Married in his late teens and the father of a son, he grew more and more restless, finally renouncing the household life in his late twenties and taking the initiative

(Erikson) to break out of the sheltered existence he had known. Cutting off his hair, Gautama donned yellow robes and began an intense six-year search for the realization of salvation. He turned first to the Brahmin philosophy, but found philosophical speculation too airy for his practical mind. He then took on the extreme bodily asceticism of Jainism, in an increasingly desperate, determined manner; for five years, under the trees of a grove at Uruvela, he literally gritted his teeth, held his breath, and tried to force enlightenment. At death's edge, common sense led Gautama to consider the possibility of a third way to salvation. Under the Bodhi tree, probably in a more relaxed reflection upon his failure, suddenly the answer came: His desire had defeated him! Achieving a lack of desire, he experienced at last the earthly foretaste of Nirvana he had so earnestly sought.

He had found a third way indeed—the middle path between the two extremes of devotion to sensual pleasures and extreme denial of sensual pleasures.[8]

That the Buddha spoke specifically of salvation and, at least indirectly, of sin, is seen in these words ascribed to him.

The brother who is arahant, in whom the intoxicants are destroyed, who has lived the life, who has done his task, who has laid low his burden, who has attained salvation, who has utterly destroyed the fetter of rebirth, who is emancipated by the true gnosis, he is incapable of perpetrating nine things:
1. He is incapable of deliberately depriving a living creature of life.
2. He is incapable of taking what is not given so that it constitutes theft.
3. He is incapable of sexual impurity.
4. He is incapable of deliberately telling lies.
5. He is incapable of laying up treasure for indulgence in worldly pleasure as he used to do in the life of the house.
6. He is incapable of taking a wrong course through partiality.
7. He is incapable of taking a wrong course through hate.
8. He is incapable of taking a wrong course through stupidity.
9. He is incapable of taking a wrong course through fear.[9]

Confucius—Sin and Redemption

Confucius, K'ungfutze, or Master King, the youngest of eleven children, was born to poor but respected parents in

STAGE THREE: INITIATIVE

the Shantung province of China. After his father's death in Confucius' early childhood, it was necessary for him to work, but he received a good education and became a lifelong student of the classical works of ancient China.

Confucius married, sired a son, and was divorced shortly thereafter. He left his minor government post of tax collector in his late twenties to establish himself as a teacher. His teachings, a sort of ethical humanism, stemmed from his belief that the moral conditions of his day were corrupt (sinful?) but not beyond redemption. The way toward salvation, according to Confucius, was to reclaim *li* (a difficult word to define but having to do with a ritualized, proper, religious, and moral way of life founded on the same principles as the Golden Rule and idealized by the ancients). If a society practices *li*, the horizontal harmony effected among the people inevitably spills over upon and enhances a vertical harmony between people and ultimates—between earth and heaven.[10]

Confucius' relationship to fathers differs from that of the other personal-religion founders. Perhaps the early death of his own father and his deep attachment to his mother (as reflected in his retirement from public life at her death, for a time greater than was customary) gave Confucius' teachings a special Oedipal twist in which he both attacked the father-structures of his day and revered the father-structures of days gone by. Consider his poignant "Plea to an Ancestor."

> Alas for me, who am a little child,
> On whom has devolved the unsettled state!
> Solitary am I and full of distress.
> Oh! my great father,
> All thy life long, thou wast filial.
> Thou didst think of my great grandfather,
> See in him, as it were, ascending and descending
>   in the count;
> I, the little child,
> Day and night will be as reverent.
> Oh! ye great kings,
> As your successor, I will strive not to forget you.

CONSCIOUSNESS AND THE ULTIMATE

Jesus—Sin and Redemption

Jesus was born to parents of a humble but self-supporting station common to the day. Growing up in Nazareth of Galilee with his brothers and probably working at the carpentry trade, he became something of a self-taught rabbi. At approximately age thirty, after his baptism by John the Baptist, he began a public ministry that differed from John's by the de-emphasis of asceticism and baptism and the emphasis upon the announcement of the coming kingdom of God on a universal scale.

Thus Jesus' teachings about sin and salvation/redemption can best be understood when seen in the light of the central focus upon the announcement of the already-arriving kingdom. The Gospel of Mark, seen by scholars as the earliest and least embellished of the four scriptural accounts of Jesus' life, contains only one incident in which he speaks about sins and their forgiveness.[11] The Gospel of Luke contains the only use of the words salvation and redemption.

In his ministry Jesus took the initiative, in the Eriksonian sense, by pushing beyond the stance of John the Baptist to challenge the formal leaders of the Jewish faith and the people themselves with his call for sincerity and complete self-commitment to preparation for the arrival of the kingdom of God. This was to be done by elevating the absolute principle of love into a predominant place, above all social, legal, and ceremonial demands.[12]

In his relationship to his family, as well as in his total ministry, Jesus demonstrated a startling exercise of personal authority to the extent that he cast aside existing norms for the behavior of a loyal son (Oedipal implications?), but on the other hand, he revealed a unique intimacy with his Father-God, as evidenced by his use of the Aramaic word *abba*, roughly translatable to the English "daddy." Consider his prayer at Gethsemane on the eve of the Crucifixion. "Abba, Father, all things are possible to thee; remove this cup from me; yet not what I will, but what thou wilt."[13]

STAGE THREE: INITIATIVE

Muhammad—Sin and Redemption

Muhammad was born in the Arabian trade-crossroads city of Mecca to a woman already widowed, whose husband had been a member of the established ruling tribe of Quraysh. She too died, and at age six, Muhammad became a ward of his grandfather and later of his uncle and faithful protector, Abu Talib.

As Muhammad grew to maturity he became increasingly disturbed by the religion (polytheism and animism) and the life-style (quarreling, drinking, gambling, dancing, and immorality) of his city. Having married a wealthy widow fifteen years his senior (to meet unfulfilled Oedipal needs?) who encouraged his religious interest, Muhammad spent more and more time brooding over the belief common to Jews and Christians of that time that there would be a last judgment by the one true God and punishment of idolators (sinners?) by everlasting fire.

While visiting a cave near Mount Hira when he was about forty, he received a vision of God's messenger, calling upon him to recite. Excited and yet only half believing, he hurried home to record the whole revelation, now a part of the Islam holy writ, the Koran. He feared for his sanity, but with the support of his wife and family, and through succeeding revelations, he came to see his role as a true prophet of the one real God, Allah.[14]

Sin was not a new idea—it was precisely what the Hanifs (penitents) of Muhammad's city had maintained for some time: Belief in the many tribal gods would lead to perdition. So it was with salvation/redemption. As the Hanifs thought, so Muhammad proclaimed: Salvation comes by *Islam*—submission to the will of the one God, Allah, plus prayers, alms-giving, and temperance.

Since the message of Muhammad was not new to the people, they were slow to respond. Gradually his preaching became more threatening; his Eriksonian initiative took the form of attacks against the Meccan establishment for its refusal to give up worship of the old gods and its unwillingness to acknowledge Muhammad's authority as the final and greatest of the Semitic prophets. Eventually his thrusts against the power structure led to his ascendancy and dominance in both the religious and the political sphere (killing the fathers?).[15] The basic credal formula given Islam by Muhammad is "(There is) no god but Allah; Muhammad is the messenger (or prophet) of Allah."[16]

Summary: A Typology of the Initiative Stage

In the ongoing process of human religious development, a particular historical moment signaled the arrival of a third stage. That historical moment begins at the estimated birth date of Zoroaster (660 B.C.), spans a millennium, and ends with the death of Muhammad in A.D. 632. It is characterized by the lives and ministries of seven men who personally founded lasting world religions: Zoroaster, Lao-tze, Mahavira, Gautama, Confucius, Jesus, and Muhammad.

Specific characteristics of this third stage are included in a composite biography of those lives, and are roughly analogous to the characteristics of individual human beings in the third psychosocial developmental crisis described by Erikson—initiative versus guilt (with implications for one's emerging doctrines of sin and salvation/redemption). Each religion founder took the initiative (in the Eriksonian sense) to sharply challenge and move beyond his given socio-economic-religious role, directly or indirectly declaring the ways of the fathers sinful (with strong Oedipal implications).

Furthermore, the seven collectively concentrated upon discovering and announcing ways to be redeemed from the sinful state of "things as they are," by meditative self-denial, harmony with natural processes, temperance, ethical responsibility, or submission to the perceived will of God, thus internalizing within the human psyche the battle between good and evil, which earlier was resolvable only on tribal battlefields.[17]

CHAPTER 5

STAGE FOUR: INDUSTRY

The Specific Hypothesis

The fourth stage, industry, has to do with the process that perpetuated and elaborated upon the insights and teachings of the seven religion-founding geniuses. By definition, then, this stage in human religious development is the institutionalization phase of the world's lasting religions and correlates with Erikson's stage of individual development.

For the West this movement toward systematization and crystallization began with the death and resurrection of Jesus and culminated with the medieval synthesis of Christendom, on the eve of the Renaissance.[1]

The massive amount of work required to nurture the faithful followers of Jesus in the face of early persecutions, to challenge the existing Greco-Roman culture and evangelize it, and then to consolidate those gains in the institutional church, is strikingly parallel to the works theme (industry is Erikson's word) in the individual development of children age six to twelve.

The child at the age of five or six enters a world where technology dominates—the schoolroom. There, along with the socialization process, the child is called upon to master the tools of technology—reading, writing, and arithmetic. There are rewards for achievement; punishment awaits failure.

The child gets the message that one is saved by good

works. In the ideal situation, the child begins to achieve in a satisfying fashion and, at the same time, balances the saved-by-works message with earlier and continuing experiences that are predominantly trusting, autonomy-affirming, and redemptive. ("I am really saved by grace, not by anything I can *do,* though it does feel good to do a good job.") Failing this, the child feels largely inferior in the psychological sense and lost in the theological sense.

The account of the work that concretely embodies the spirit and the message of the founding religious geniuses (from this point, limited to Jesus) in permanent, increasingly formal religious structures (from this point, limited to the church), is in part a projection onto the historical screen of the works-oriented latency period in individual human development.

The Work of Pioneering the Kingdom of God

"Now after John was arrested, Jesus came into Galilee, preaching the gospel of God, and saying, 'The time is fulfilled, and the kingdom of God is at hand; repent, and believe in the gospel.' "[2] That Jesus opened his public ministry with the announcement that the kingdom (or reign) of God was near and that he later sent his disciples out to make the proclamation, is widely accepted. One New Testament scholar holds that the kingdom of God was the central theme of the teaching of Jesus.[3] That term or an equivalent is found thirteen times in Mark, thirteen in Q Source, twenty-five in Matthew, and six in Luke.[4]

The many parables of the kingdom, especially the petition "thy kingdom come" in the Lord's Prayer, point up Jesus' thought that the coming of the kingdom had yet to be consummated. But the process had already begun. "The kingdom of God is not coming with signs to be observed; nor will they say 'Lo, here it is!' or 'There!' for behold, the kingdom of God is in the midst of you."[5]

In describing religion as an institution, Alan Wells defines the prophetic role: The prophet proclaims a new message; he regards himself as one who has a duty to proclaim to humankind this new message from the gods or from God.[6]

STAGE FOUR: INDUSTRY

Although Jesus did make use of the language and ideas of the apocalyptic visionaries of his day, quite unlike them, he refused to elaborate portraits of the glories of heaven or the horrors of hell. For Jesus, the coming of the kingdom was beyond calculation and dependent only upon God's will, hidden in the ordinary present, where no one is aware of what is taking place.[7]

This is a fresh vision—a truly prophetic message—a breakthrough to a higher order, by a charismatic leader.[8] This is the stuff of which mass movements are made, according to Eric Hoffer.

> The preliminary work of undermining existing institutions, of familiarizing the masses with the idea of change, and of creating a receptivity to a new faith, can be done only by men who are, first and foremost, talkers or writers and are recognized as such by all.[9]

Jesus is a prime example of Wells' prophet, Weber's charismatic leader, Hoffer's man of words. However, prophetic leadership is essentially personal and impermanent. Upon the death of the leader, the task becomes one of institutionalization.

> Religious institutionalization is essentially the attempt to develop that degree of permanence necessary to guarantee the continuity of the group and its beliefs. The institutionalized religious group becomes increasingly formal, organized, influential within society, inclusive, authoritarian, distant from original beliefs, and ecumenical.[10]

This institutionalization process now becomes the focus in the study of the industry phase of Christian history.

The Work of Materializing the Kingdom of God

> And now, behold, I am going to Jerusalem, bound in the Spirit, not knowing what shall befall me there; except that the Holy Spirit testifies to me in every city that imprisonment and afflictions await me. But I do not account my life of any value nor as precious to myself, if only I may accomplish my course and the ministry which I received from the Lord Jesus, to testify to the gospel of the grace of God. And now, behold, I know that all you among whom I have gone preaching the kingdom will see my face no more.[11]

CONSCIOUSNESS AND THE ULTIMATE

These words of the apostle Paul, spoken to the elders of the church at Ephesus, capsule Paul's total dedication, even beyond concern for his life, to the work of announcing and interpreting the kingdom of God as begun by his Lord, Jesus. A first-century Jew and a persecutor of Jesus' followers, Paul was transformed by his experience on the Damascus Road into the leading missionary of early Christianity. His works are astounding. Almost single-handedly, he introduced the message of Jesus to the northwestern Mediterranean world by establishing churches in many key cities, thereby releasing that message from its Jewish limits and giving it universal relevance.[12]

In the development of religious institutions, Wells would see Paul's role as that of evangelist. A lieutenant, rather than a prophet, Wells' evangelist travels, leads classes, encourages fellow believers, and generally supports the continuing work of a fledgling sect, thus fulfilling an essential function in its young life.[13]

For Weber, the rise of a religious community is the result of what he calls routinization, a process in which either the prophet or the prophet's disciples make his preaching permanent and the congregation's distribution of grace stable, thus insuring both the economic existence of the budding institution and the reason-for-being of those who maintain it.[14]

Hoffer has chosen a sharp, emotion-laden term. "When the moment is ripe, only the *fanatic* can hatch a genuine mass movement."[15] Hoffer theorizes that fanatics come from the ranks of noncreative men of words. Whereas creative men of words find fulfillment in creative work, fanatics do not. Whereas creative men of words are at heart reformers, fanatics are at their core destroyers. Whereas creative men of words tend to blanch at the chaos their words suggest, fanatics thrive on eternal flux, intuitively knowing that their own inner chaos can never be completely ordered. Hoffer cites Marat, Robespierre, Lenin, Mussolini, and Hitler as historical examples.

It would be gross oversimplification to imply that Paul and Paul alone bridged the gap between Jesus-in-the-flesh and the embryo church; the New Testament and the earliest

STAGE FOUR: INDUSTRY

traditions recount the accomplishments of countless heroes and heroines in the Christian confrontation with the established Roman-dominated order. Churches sprang up and flourished despite, or probably because of, persecution.

External factors contributing to the spread of Christianity included the Pax Romana and its accompanying network of roads and trade routes, which enhanced travel and communication; a more or less uniform Greek culture and language; the fading power of the current mystery religions; and the A.D. 70 fall of Jerusalem, with the resulting dispersion of its inhabitants throughout the Empire.

Some internal reasons for Christianity's spread were belief in the resurrection of Jesus, the ready availability of God's Holy Spirit, confidence in the early return of Jesus Christ, the strong sense of brother/sisterhood among believers, and the centrality of Christ as Lord.

Organizationally, the work of materializing the kingdom of God can be seen in the development of the role and power of the bishop. During the first century A.D. the collegiate bishop shared leadership with other bishops within a single congregation, and the titles of bishop, elder, and pastor seem to have been used interchangeably. In the second century, a monarchical bishop emerged to take clear leadership responsibility within most of the congregations. Diocesan bishops, toward whom several neighboring congregations looked for authoritative direction, became evident in the historical record during the third century. By the fourth century, leading churches' metropolitan bishops had consolidated even wider authority and power. The fifth century evolved five leading patriarchs—the bishops of Rome, Constantinople, Alexandria, Antioch, and Jerusalem.[16]

There were some key events in the establishment of Christianity: the Edict of Milan (312), placing Christianity on a par with other religions; the consolidation of power by the first Christian Roman emperor, Constantine (323); and the declaration by Theodosius (380) that Christianity was to be the sole religion of the Empire.

Perhaps the words of Augustine (354–430), Bishop of Hippo, reflect and symbolize as well as any other the full materialization of the kingdom of God. Although the point could be denied today by some Roman Catholic theologians, Augustine seems to use the terms "kingdom of God" and "Church" interchangeably.

Writing on the subject "What the reign of the saints with Christ for a thousand years is, and how it differs from the eternal kingdom," he makes the following statements.

> We must understand in one sense the kingdom of heaven in which exist together both he who breaks what he teaches and he who does it, the one being least, the other great, and in another sense the kingdom of heaven into which only he who does what he teaches shall enter. Consequently, where both classes exist, it is the Church as it now is, but where only the one shall exist, it is the Church as it is destined to be when no wicked person shall be in her. Therefore the Church even now is the kingdom of Christ, and the kingdom of heaven.[17]

The Work of Consolidating the Kingdom of God

Innocent I (401–417) vies with Leo I (440–461) and Gregory I (590–604) for the title of first pope, in terms of preeminence over other churches and the consolidation of power and authority in the Church of Rome. In a toss-up, Innocent I becomes the beginning point for this section, not only because his dates of service as Bishop of Rome make him a contemporary of Augustine, but also because, in this account of a "works" stage in the development of the human religious consciousness as expressed in Christian history, Innocent I was known for his industriousness. He claimed not only custody of the apostolic tradition and the foundation of all Western Christianity for the Roman Church, but also used the decisions of Sardica as a basis upon which to claim universal jurisdiction for the Roman bishop.[18]

Thus he represents, in a dramatic fashion, Wells' priestly role in religious institutional development. For Wells, the priest is essentially a performer of ceremony, charged with certain sacred powers for the performance of his duties by an authoritarian type of religious organization. Whereas the prophet is seen as something more than an ordinary human being, the priest is not. The priest's powers are those of the office, not of the person, and are quite independent of a

STAGE FOUR: INDUSTRY

good or evil personality.[19] Weber saw this office as centering upon the ritualized institutional dispensation of salvation.[20] Hoffer calls such an officer the man of action.

> The man of action saves the movement from the suicidal dissensions and the recklessness of the fanatics. But his appearance usually marks the end of the dynamic phase of the movement. The war with the present is over. The genuine man of action is intent not on renovating the world but on possessing it.[21]

And so the "men of action" worked to do just that, through monasticism, the Councils, the Crusades, the orders, the ascendency of the papacy, and Scholasticism.

The greatest of the Scholastics, Thomas Aquinas (1225–1274), gave Pope Boniface VIII (1294–1303) the theological basis for the high-water claim of papal authority over civil matters, the famous bull *Unam sanctum*. In it the Pope, citing the opinion of Aquinas, declared "that it is altogether necessary to salvation for every human being to be subject to the Roman pontiff."[22] The medieval synthesis known as Christendom had been achieved![23]

Summary: A Typology of the Industry Stage

The fourth stage in the development of human religious consciousness comprises the work of permanently establishing the insights, the teachings, the charisma of the founding religious geniuses. This institutionalization process corresponds to the fourth psychosocial individual developmental crisis, called by Erikson industry versus inferiority, in which the doctrine of works is being learned at the feeling level.

In a narrowing of scope, this study now centers on the crystallization of Christianity as a prime historical illuminative case of the works stage. The pioneering work of Jesus (the kingdom of God as the imminent reign of God) evolved in the materializing work of Paul and Augustine (the kingdom of God as interchangeable with church) and in the consolidating work of Aquinas and Boniface VIII (the kingdom of God equals the world), toward its culmination in Christendom (the medieval synthesis).

CHAPTER 6

STAGE FIVE: IDENTITY

The Specific Hypothesis

The rise of science and humanism, beginning with the Renaissance and continuing to the present, marks a fifth stage, in which the central questions are those of identity. Who am I? To whom am I accountable? What are the limits, if any, of my authority, wisdom, and power? This fifth stage, with emphasis on humanity coming into its own—literally coming of age—is seen as the adolescence of Western religious consciousness.

In the adolescence of individuals, beginning with the onset of puberty and continuing to full bodily maturity near the end of the "teen" years, the questions are the same. What does it mean to be human? A man? A woman? A sexual being with adult physical and mental capabilities?

There is a movement away from the once total infantile dependence upon parents, toward total adult independence, often occurring in uneven spurts, leaving both the adolescent and the parents baffled, angry, and exhausted. The adolescent's peer group replaces parent and hero as a model for the dress, values, and activities that are important. Dating and endless conversation among youth help to clarify and explore the meanings and feelings associated with developing sexuality. Vocational choices must be narrowed, if not specifically settled, and accompanying educational plans must be made and carried out.

Religiously, the battle for individual independence often

STAGE FIVE: IDENTITY

takes place in the arena of churchgoing and/or religious beliefs. Parent-gods and God are easily blurred; a need to test independence from parents may focus upon God. An announcement of atheism to devout parents, or of religious dedication to nonreligious parents both may be expressions of the same need—to gain enough distance from parents and the parentally given faith (or lack of faith) to discover what it is like to be on one's own—to stand on one's own two feet. This is not to say that such announcements can be completely psychologized as mere emotional distancing. Indeed, the adolescent is moving toward full adult capacity to think abstractly and critically. From a purely intellectual standpoint, such critical analyses and their accompanying choices are age-appropriate.

Historically in the West, the battle for independence took place over against the maternalism of Mother Church and the paternalism of the Holy Father, who had carefully regulated the totality of life in the medieval synthesis and had said in effect, "We know best. We'll take care of everything for you. Just do exactly as we say, be good children, and your reward will be great in the next life. Those of you who disobey, risk excommunication, death, and hellfire!"

The Coming of Age in Its Scientific Expression

The coming divergence between the world of belief and the world of science was not anticipated. As late as 1691, *The Wisdom of God Manifested in the Works of the Creation*, published by John Ray, continued the assumption that investigation of the physical universe would merely reveal more of the ways in which God cares for man. Yet hints were there. "That the height of the mountains doth continually diminish is very likely," faintly glimpsed erosion as a power at work in nature over millions of years, not accounted for in Archbishop Ussher's calculations from biblical genealogies, that Creation took place in 4004 B.C.

By 1691 many forces and events had been undermining the citadel of Christendom: the Crusades, which encouraged trade, communication, and an influx of heretical ideas; the invention of the movable-type printing press, which gave access to accumulated wisdom outside the cloister; the wave of exploration, which resulted in the ordinary mind's perception of the world as a globe; the Copernican revolution, which perceived a heliocentric universe; and the work of Vesalius in anatomy, of Gilbert with magnetism and electricity, of Harvey with the discovery of the circulation of blood. Loren Eiseley lifts up two events—the discovery of the speed of light and Newton's formulation of the laws of gravity—as pivotal.

Though the discovery was slow to make its impact, Roemer's 1675 notice of a slight lag in the reappearance of one of Jupiter's moons after an eclipse, led to calculations fixing the speed of light at 186,000 miles per second. The way was now open to the light year as a means of encompassing astronomical time.

Newton, a devoutly religious man, provided, with his laws of gravity, the single weight in Kepler's description of the universe as "something like a clockwork in which a single weight drives all the gears." Unaware, Newton thereby laid the groundwork of the introduction of cosmic evolution by Kant and Laplace. Eiseley puts it poetically: "The wheels and cogs of the celestial machine for the first time would be pursued backward until they dissolved in spinning vapor."[1]

Using Newtonian mathematics and bringing the Kant-Laplace cosmic evolution theory home to earth, Hutton challenged the popular geological theory of catastrophism. He began, not with a cataclysmic creation event, but with the earth as he found it. Noticing a bit of soil carried down a mountain brook, the wind constantly eroding and polishing mountain crags, he came upon the secret of the constant youth of the world—time and rain drops. Gradualism had replaced catastrophism in geology.[2]

From the naturalization of the cosmos, to that of the earth, to the desacralization of the earth's creatures, including human beings, is a logical progression. And Darwin, using the insights of those who went before him as well as the findings from his Beagle voyage, made that association with his evolutionary concept of natural selection. Yet Eiseley, the scientist, finds it in himself to write about that desacralization process in summary:

> "Natural" is a magician's word—and like all such entities, it should be used sparingly lest there arise from it, as now, some unglimpsed, unintended world, some monstrous caricature called into being by the indiscreet articulation of worn syllables.
>
> Man, at last, is face to face with himself in natural guise. "What we make natural, we destroy," said Pascal. He knew, with superlative insight, man's complete necessity to transcend the worldly image that this word connotes.[3]

Even this brief sketch of humanity's coming of age in its scientific expression would be incomplete without mention of Einstein's 1905 discovery of relativity, the impact of which includes the surpassing of the absolutes of Newtonian physics and the unleashing of the power of the atom. The full implications of relativity even now remain unexplored.

> From a formal point of view one may characterize the achievement of the special theory of relativity thus: it has shown generally the role which the universal constant c (velocity of light) plays in the laws of nature and has demonstrated that there exists a close connection between the form in which time on the one hand and the spatial coordinates on the other hand enter into the laws of nature.[4]

The Coming of Age in Its Philosphical Expression

Francis Bacon (1561–1626), an Elizabethan curiously ahead of his time, became one of the first philosophers of the emerging scientific world-view. Writing in *The Advancement of Learning,* Bacon distills into one sentence the essence of the coming science. "This is the foundation of all, for we are not to imagine or suppose, but to *discover*, what nature does or may be made to do." Seen within the intellectual context of that age of semiliteracy with its emphasis upon revival of classic Greek and Roman literature, such a distillation is impressively prophetic. His was a call away from Scholasticism's deduction of general laws and principles, toward induction from a patient collection of observed facts.[5]

Benedict Spinoza (1632–1682), a Jew from the Netherlands, excommunicated at age twenty-four because of his ideas that God might have a body (matter), that angels might be hallucinations, that the soul might be merely life, and that the Old Testament says nothing about immortality, passed his days in serene solitude, grinding lenses and attempting to unify Descartes' mind-and-matter dichotomy. This he set forth in *A Theologico-Political Treatise*, by forcefully challenging, in the popular mind, the Cartesian separation of the power of God from the power of nature. He held that the two are one, and more clearly seen as such when the Bible is properly interpreted by taking into consideration its textual origins, authorship, purpose, and historical context.[6] Where Francis Bacon lifted up the objective and realistic, Spinoza synthesized it with Cartesian subjective idealism into a determinism, which no longer presents God as a "capricious personality absorbed in the private affairs of his devotees, but [as] the invariable sustaining order of the universe."[7]

Voltaire (1694–1778) has been characterized as the soul of the eighteenth century. Poet, playwright, caustic wit, darling of the aristocracy, and occasional occupant of the Bastille, he speaks for himself and for the French Enlightenment in the following excerpts from his works.

Our priests are not what simple folk suppose;
Their learning is but our credulity.

Let us trust to ourselves, see all with our own eyes;
Let these be our oracles, our tripods and our gods.

True prayer lies not in asking for a violation of natural law but in the acceptance of natural law as the unchangeable will of God.[8]

The Prussian professor of philosophy Immanuel Kant (1724–1804), with his *Critique of Pure Reason* (1781), dominated the thought of the nineteenth century as Voltaire had that of the eighteenth. In essence, its eight hundred pages saved science by limiting its applications to the surface world and its appearances. But religion, too, was saved by the argument that the objects of faith—namely, a free and immortal soul, as well as a benevolent Creator never could be proved by reason. Then since religion cannot be based on science or theology, it must be based on morals generally and on an absolute categorical imperative in particular—duty.[9]

The thought of German philosopher Friedrich Nietzsche (1844–1900) represents the culmination of the humanist thrust in the idea of the superman. His Zarathustra (a metaphorical reincarnation of Zoroaster, who, since he had introduced the idea of moral good and evil, was selected as the appropriate figure to move beyond moral good and evil) was the spokesman for the superman idea. The ethical imperative of the superman is to become what one is—a higher man—through severe self-discipline and honest self-knowledge. Such men, now beyond good and evil, would have new values as a direct result of the will to power, the enjoyment of the here and now, and full acceptance of the innocence of existence.

Nietzsche saw the Christian church of the medieval synthesis as completely corrupt and impotent. Its holy hatreds, sacred dogmas, denunciations, and even its God, Nietzsche angrily pronounced as dead.[10] With that announcement, philosophically at least, Western humanity had its basis for a thoroughgoing desacralization, a total secularization—a coming of age—in the sense that the late adolescent makes the break from home to take his place in the adult world.

The Coming of Age in Its Political Expression

By the time of the medieval synthesis, intertribal relations in Europe had evolved into the elaborate system of feudalism, with its intricate laws and customs. The most powerful chieftain (known as a nobleman or lord) in a given area demanded political allegiance from lesser lords, in return for guarantees of protection against outside aggressors.

As power was broadened and consolidated at the top levels of nobility, feudal monarchies emerged under the leadership of kings, at least in western Europe. By the late fifteenth century, the prototype of today's national states had appeared in Spain, France, and England, through expansion by warfare, marriage, or inheritance.[11]

For the two centuries following 1450, increasing areas of the world came under the domination of European nations through adventurous (early adolescent?) explorers who claimed the territories they discovered in the name of the monarchs they served. Colonies developed. Kings became emperors, with absolute royal authority.

But this absolute authority of the political fathers (mothers, of course, in the instance of empresses) was assaulted by the ordinary people across and beyond the European continent with varying degrees of success, in what can be seen as a late-adolescent political coming of age. First through the rise of parliamentary government in England and later through the American, French, and Russian revolutions, human beings attempted to wrest control of their own destinies from the benevolent/malevolent hands of a privileged minority who thought they knew best how to run a world and that they had a divine right to do so.

The struggle continues today, joined recently by adolescents, the poor, and third-world citizens, in what Erikson calls a unified revolt of the dependent, precipitated by enhanced transportation, communication, and increasing affluence.[12]

The Coming of Age in Its Economic Expression

Parallel to the consolidation of small political entities into larger and more powerful states was the accompanying unification of economic systems and the expansion of world trade. Through the fortuitous combination in eighteenth-century England of market availability, risk capital provided by adventurous entrepreneurs, ample labor supply, available raw materials, and technical ability, the Industrial Revolution got under way. It massively increased humankind's power to control the materials of nature. Machines began to mass-produce cloth, steel, and steam; the wireless, roads, canals, and railroads shrank distances; the factory system was about to replace the craftsman.

But this was only the beginning. Midway through the nineteenth century, industrialization entered a second phase in which its impact was felt more fully in power politics. Production methods were improved in established industries. New industries sprang up. Newly industrialized nations (Germany, the U.S., and Russia) challenged Great Britain, France, and Belgium in world markets. Capitalism refused to honor political boundaries; its excesses almost immediately produced reactions, including those of Marx and Engels, as expressed in the *Communist Manifesto*. Humankind had arrived in modernity, fully muscled with an industrial technology.

The Coming of Age in Its Theological Expression

The coming of age of Western humanity in the religious dimension was precipitated by the ideas and technology literally unleashed in the other dimensions just capsuled (and some not described, including the artistic and psychological). The church hung on tenaciously to the peaceful, orderly status quo of the medieval synthesis as long as possible, resisting and denying the new ideas and discoveries that threatened it.

But the unquestioned authority of Mother Church and Holy Father was eroding from within, as well as from external pressures. A growing critical voice had been heard since the time of Erasmus (1466–1536), who, as a dedicated Christian, condemned asceticism, superstition, formalism, and hypocrisy within the Church and advocated living a normal secular life.[13] (For purposes of this study the Reformation is seen basically as an attempt to maintain the status quo by purification, and therefore not particularly important in the coming of age as expressed in the secularization process.)

William Blake (1757–1827) discovered in Jesus a symbolic individual, exemplifying what every individual might become—a potential divinity available to everyone!

CONSCIOUSNESS AND THE ULTIMATE

> The vision of Christ that thou dost see
> Is my Visions Greatest Enemy
> Thine has a great hook nose like thine
> Mine has a snub nose like to mine
> Thine is the friend of All Mankind
> Mine speaks in parables to the Blind
> Thine loves the same world that mine hates
> Thy Heaven doors are my Hell Gates
> Socrates taught what Melitus
> Loathed as a Nations bitterest Curse
> And Caiphas was in his own Mind
> A benefactor to Mankind
> Both read the Bible day and night
> But thou readst black where I read white.[14]

Friedrich Schleiermacher (1768–1834) believed the concept of God as a single being outside and behind the world to be inadequate. "The true nature of religion is . . . immediate consciousness of the Deity as He is found in ourselves and in the world."[15]

George W. F. Hegel (1770–1831) saw Christ as "the unifying resolution of the dialectical contradiction between spirit and matter, between God and man."[16] Soren Kierkegaard (1813–1855), regarded by some as the father of existentialism, thought the Christian life impeded by the trappings of institutional religion. He held that the vital issue is not transcendence versus immanence, but rather existence versus essence: Christianity is a way to be, not a set of opinions. When near death, and asked if he wished to receive Communion, he replied, "Yes, but not from a parson. . . .Royal functionaries are not related to Christianity."[17]

Secular literary critical tools began to be utilized to judge Scripture. Wellhausen and Strauss applied higher and textual criticism techniques to the Bible in an orderly study of authorship, historical context, and literary style. Ernest Renan (1823–1892), best known for writing the first critically oriented life of Jesus, joined the increasing call for secularization.

Now, the return to religion can be nothing else than the return to the great unity of life, to the religion of the intellect without

STAGE FIVE: IDENTITY

exclusion and without limit. The sage has no need of praying at certain hours, for his whole life is a prayer. If religion is to have a distinct place in life it must absorb life altogether.[18]

Paul Tillich (1886–1965) spoke of God as the ground of being; of the God above the God of theism; and of the courage to be rooted in the God who appears after the God of theism has disappeared in the anxiety of doubt. " 'God' is the answer to the question implied in man's finitude; he is the name for that which concerns man ultimately."[19]

Dietrich Bonhoeffer (1906–1945), in a Nazi prison, wrote of a powerless God who allowed himself to be edged out of the world and onto a cross. He called for the practice of a religionless Christianity, in which one lives without having God as a working hypothesis.[20]

But the ultimate step in secularization was taken when theologians themselves announced the death of God. The names of Paul van Buren, William Hamilton, Gabriel Vahanian, as well as those of Harvey Cox and John A. T. Robinson, are associated with this movement, which surfaced into the popular consciousness briefly in the 1960s. The boldest by far is Thomas J. J. Altizer.

The radical Christian proclaims that God has actually died in Christ, that this death is both a historical and a cosmic event, and, as such, it is a final and irrevocable event, which cannot be reversed by a subsequent religious or cosmic movement. True, a religious reversal of the death of God has indeed occurred in history, is present in the religious expressions of Christianity, and is now receding into the mist of an archaic, if not soon to be forgotten past. But such a religious reversal cannot annul the event of the death of God; it cannot recover the living God of the old covenant, nor can it reverse or bring to an end the progressive descent of Spirit into flesh.[21]

Summary: A Typology of the Identity Stage

The fifth stage in Western religious development, initiated by the Renaissance men who shattered the peace of Christendom's medieval synthesis with such questions as, Who am I? and, What are my limits? introduced the growth

CONSCIOUSNESS AND THE ULTIMATE

of science and humanism that continues today in a manner analogous to adolescence in individual development.

Even as the emerging adult challenges and eventually moves beyond his parents, so did Western humanity challenge and eventually begin to move beyond Mother Church and Holy Father, scientifically, philosophically, politically, economically, artistically, psychologically, and theologically.

CHAPTER 7

STAGE SIX: INTIMACY

The Specific Hypothesis

The process of secularization (analogous to adolescence in individual human development), begun with the Renaissance in Western civilization, continues to run its course past the crumbled walls of the Christendom of medieval synthesis. It claims ever more of the territory which once was the unquestioned domain of a now-deceased Oriental-despot God, by explaining scientifically more and more of the mysteries of the universe.

A fierce release of atomic power in the sky over Hiroshima in August 1945, thrust mankind into a sixth stage of religious development, parallel to that of individuals in early adulthood, the intimacy stage, even before secularization had run its full course. Here the individual issue is, How do I get close to another person without losing my own identity? Globally, the question needs only slight revision, with four underlying factors now shockingly apparent.

1. The history of man runs in the direction of a unity of humanity in the sense of a common destiny.
2. The history of man runs in the direction of an acceleration in the rhythm of experience.
3. An increasing gap, with accompanying tensions, is widening between man's outward freedom via technical ability and man's humaneness, or goodness.

CONSCIOUSNESS AND THE ULTIMATE

4. Man now has the technical means to destroy all men in a matter of a few moments.[1]

The religious doctrine in focus for most western individuals in early adulthood is Christology. Whatever else Jesus Christ was and is to individuals, he provides a model of intimacy by living a life so well-grounded and centered in a unique sense of identity that he was able to share intimately, with many people, at many levels, with great spontaneity and meaning, while on his undeviating way to his own destiny.

In this sixth stage in the developing religious consciousness of humankind, the symbol of a resurrected Christ becomes central, now loosed as a God-presence in the world, after the irreversible death of the Oriental-despot God who ruled from his throne "up there." This is especially so when the acceleration-in-the-rhythm-of-experience factor's full impact upon the sequence of Eriksonian stages is appreciated. Consider the very roughly estimated correlation depicted in the following chart.

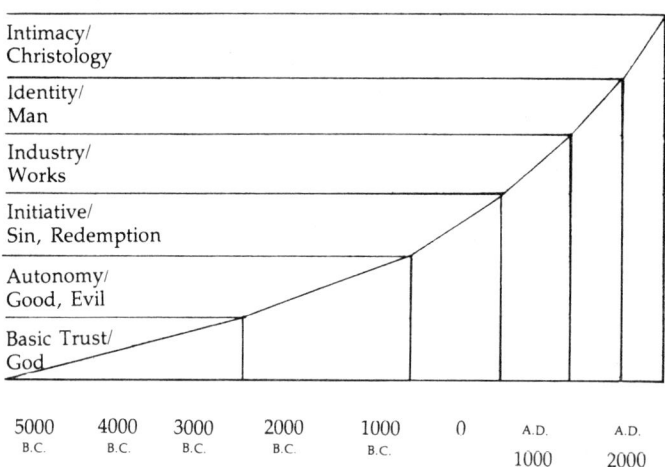

Suddenly not one but *both* the remaining Eriksonian stages loom ahead of Spaceship Earth on the temporal horizon, hurtling toward us (or rather, we toward them),

STAGE SIX: INTIMACY

not in sequence, but side by side as alternatives, as the chart line projected beyond the intimacy/christology stage becomes increasingly vertical.

The remainder of this chapter will elaborate the hypothesis related to the intimacy stage—the present state of affairs. The next chapters will examine the two options facing humankind—the generativity alternative versus the integrity choice.

Intimacy in Its Demographic Dimension

Intimacy as sheer proximity was seen as a potential problem first by Thomas Malthus in his prophetic 1798 work, *An Essay on the Principle of Population.* His thesis was that the population, unchecked, increases in a geometric ratio, while subsistence increases only in an arithmetic ratio.[2] Statistics vividly bear him out in the geometric progression of population. The population of the world reached the 500 million mark about A.D. 1650. Estimates are that it had taken 1,000 years to double itself. Within 200 years, by 1850 (thanks in large measure to the rise of medical science with skyrocketing birthrates and plummeting death rates), it had doubled again to a billion people. The next doubling interval was 80 years, as the population reached the 2 billion mark about 1930.[3] At the middle of 1974 it stood at 4,061,100,000.[4] The doubling time had been reduced to less than 45 years. Estimates at this writing peg the current doubling rate of the population of the world at about 35 years.[5] The mind boggles at any projection of figures beyond the immediate future at this rate.

A set of additionally discomfiting statistics accompanies that of the basic doubling population rate. Whereas doubling times in the industrial countries such as the United States, Russia, and Japan fall in the 50- to 200-year range, those of the underdeveloped countries are between 20 and 35 years. Furthermore, over 40 percent of the people in the underdeveloped countries are under 15 years of age, just ready to move into their reproductive years.[6]

Those who have a professional vested interest in the

reduction of the rate of population growth claim success in arresting the world birthrate. A chart widely distributed by the United States Agency for International Development depicts that 72 out of 82 of those countries with good vital statistics have had a decrease in their percent of birthrate since 1960. This picture is sharply challenged by The Environmental Fund, which claims that the phrase "good vital statistics" greatly biases the results: Countries omitted from the list contain more than half the people in the world (The People's Republic of China, India, Pakistan, Bangladesh, and Nigeria).[7]

The distinct boundaries between "us" and "them" are rapidly blurring in an intimacy crisis of sheer numbers, leaving a burgeoning mass of ever-more-crowded fellow travelers huddling together on Spaceship Earth, with the increasingly difficult task of living a life "so well-grounded and centered in a unique sense of identity" that we are "able to share intimately, with many people, at many levels, with great spontaneity and meaning," while on the way to our respective destinies.

Intimacy in Its Ecological Dimension

The last half of the Malthusian thesis—that subsistence increases only in an arithmetic ratio—now modified by the phrase "up to the limits of growth," becomes the focal point of this discussion. The question here is, What has been the impact of exponential population growth upon the earth's physical resources, including arable land, food, raw materials, fossil and nuclear fuels, and the ecological systems that absorb wastes and recycle important basic chemical substances?

The United Nations Food and Agriculture Organization estimates that basic caloric and especially protein requirements in the underdeveloped countries are not being met; one-third of the world's people are inadequately nourished. Although only half the world's land suitable for use is under cultivation, immense capital investments would be required to reach, clear, fertilize, and irrigate the other half, making it economically prohibitive.[8]

STAGE SIX: INTIMACY

In the matter of natural resources, research of The Club of Rome/Massachusetts Institute of Technology team led to the following statement.

> Given present resource consumption rates and the projected increase in these rates, the great majority of the currently important nonrenewable resources will be extremely costly 100 years from now. The above statement remains true regardless of the most optimistic assumptions about undiscovered reserves, technological advances, substitution, or recycling, as long as the demand for resources continues to grow exponentially.[9]

As for the ecological systems that absorb wastes and recycle chemical ingredients, studies seem inconclusive, but some tentative points were reached by the team.

1. The few kinds of pollution that actually have been measured over time seem to be increasing exponentially.
2. We have almost no knowledge about where the upper limits of these pollution growth curves might be.
3. The delay in natural ecological processes increases the probability of underestimating the control measures necessary, and therefore of inadvertently reaching those upper limits.
4. Many pollutants are globally distributed; their harmful effects appear long distances from their points of generation.[10]

The distinct boundaries between "us" and "them" begin to blur in the ecological dimension as well as in the demographic, as the impact of certain facts begins to be realized—such as the 300 percent yearly increase in lead deposits in Greenland ice and the accumulation of DDT in the body fat of Alaskan Eskimos, as well as in that of citizens of New Delhi.[11]

Intimacy in Its Economic Dimension

The two great socioeconomic systems of influence in the world are capitalism and socialism. Capitalism, wherein a

CONSCIOUSNESS AND THE ULTIMATE

minority class privately owns the means of production, and the market system determines the income of production and distributes its output, is also a social order which features a drive-for-wealth-oriented middle class.

Neither of the two major predictions about capitalism—the Marxist (that of collapse through revolution by the working class) or the Keynesian (that of economic success and increasing social well-being)—has been fully realized. An increase in per capita output and an expansion of social-welfare policies did occur. But all-out revolution did not. Nor, on the other hand, did complete social harmony.[12]

Socialism, defined by the replacement of private with public ownership and of the free market with planning, has three distinct social expressions. First is the industrial socialism characteristic of the U.S.S.R. Second is the socialist order represented in some underdeveloped countries, with the same political centralization, but without the industrial framework. Third, the most tentative of the three, is the Yugoslavia-type attempt to combine high industrialization with decentralization of political control.

As with the incomplete fulfillment of the prognoses for capitalism, so too with the predictions about industrial socialism (U.S.S.R. variety). Neither the first prediction (that industrial socialism would collapse because it is inherently irrational) or the second (public ownership would usher in an age of high social morale) came to pass. So far there has been no collapse; in fact, by strictly economic criteria, industrial socialism has been about as successful as capitalism. But judging from worker morale campaigns, occasional outbreaks of worker revolt, and the continued blocking of emigration to capitalist countries, it is not yet an age of high social morale, either. What is striking is

> the surpassing similarity of outcomes between two otherwise widely differing systems. Each has been marked with serious operational difficulties; each has overcome these difficulties with economic growth. Each has succeeded in raising its level of material consumption; each has been unable to produce a climate of social satisfaction.[13]

STAGE SIX: INTIMACY

Thus the theme of a blurring of the boundaries between "us" and "them" appears in a third dimension. Each of these two great systems, once at opposite ends of the socioeconomic spectrum and declared mortal enemies, seems to be taking on some characteristics of the other and, in an intimacy of sorts, each seems to be responding with essentially the same degree of limited success to the hazards of population growth and other external dangers.

Intimacy in Its Political Dimension

Heilbroner, in his analysis of the political situation, confesses to an inability to assess meaningfully the political present, much less the future, because political fortunes are so closely bound to the personalities and idiosyncrasies of political leaders. But he does lift up two qualities learned in the extended dependency period of childhood which have special significance for the political dimension—the trait of obedience and the capacity for identification.[14]

With respect to obedience, he sees (along with the presence of force, differential social conditioning, the unequal distribution of personality characteristics, and hierarchical orderings) the deep need of human beings for a sense of psychological security as central to what he calls "the perplexing readiness, even eagerness, with which authority is accepted by the vast majority." This human tendency has important political implications. It indicates that revolutionary regimes probably will be able to promote equality for the masses only through leaders empowered with great authority—for example, Chairman Mao in China. It also means that democratic governments can meet the demands of crisis best via centralized (presumably temporary) authority vested in the persons of powerful parent-figure leaders (an extremely difficult task in a democracy).[15]

In the matter of the second human quality of special political significance—the capacity for identification—Heilbroner sees there the root of all the possibilities for human morality, as well as a seemingly inevitable limit beyond which the capacity for identification is blocked. From family to tribe to nation, we have been able to roll back the boundary distinguishing "us" from "them." So far, at least, it has not been possible to include those of another culture among "us" in any historical political situation. The positive element Heilbroner sees in the human capacity for identification (with its apparent endings at national boundary lines) lies in the mobilizing effect it can and does have on nations—especially the developing nations.[16]

Though not overly optimistic, Heilbroner sees one possibility of transcending this nationalistic us/them limit. That possibility is the ability of the people of today to form a collective bond of identity with the generations of the future—our children and our children's children. However, it is absolutely vital to any mitigation of the massive problems of the future to begin the bonding process now.[17]

Not only does the us/them dichotomy and its potential blurring appear in the political dimension. At least one voice, that of Heilbroner, is raised in an urgent call to "us" to transcend our traditional resistance to identification with "them" in the framework of time. This is an immediate and absolutely necessary step toward the solution of increasingly critical world problems.

Intimacy in Its Philosophical Dimension

Under the microscope of the linguistic philosophy of Ludwig Wittgenstein (1889–1951), even the meanings of the words us and them blur and merge. For to Wittgenstein, words

> are like tools; their functions differ from one another as much as those of a saw and a screwdriver. But their dissimilarities of function are hidden by their uniform appearance in sound and in print. The similarity between words of different kinds make us assimilate them all to names, and tempts us to try to explain their meaning by pointing to objects for which they stand.[18]

STAGE SIX: INTIMACY

Words are not understandable outside the context of the nonlinguistic human-activities fabric into which the use of language is woven. Words plus these behavioral surroundings make up language-games. The only way, then, to understand the meaning of a word is to study it within the context of its language-game, to see just how it contributes to the activities—the communal life—of its users. In other words, a word's meaning is not an object for which it stands, but its use as a language.

The most common form of philosophical nonsense arises not when a word is being used outside any language-game at all, but when it is used in a language-game other than the one appropriate to it. So it is clearly important to be able to know where one language-game ends and another begins.[19]

The implication of this philosophy of language for the study of consciousness of the ultimate is that the medieval synthesis provided an elaborate yet tightly structured context in which the God-talk of Christendom became most fully developed. As adolescent secularization swept over the Scholastic ramparts, the meanings so automatically associated in the medieval language-game with such words as God, good and evil, sin and redemption, works, man, Jesus Christ, Creation, eschatology, us, and them, were washed away, leaving a diffusion of meanings.

The meanings of the words "us" and "them" break down under the logical scrutiny of the linguistic analysis of Wittgenstein. The implications are that with the death of the language-game of Christendom, there is a great need to translate old God-talk into language meaningful within the context of the new intimacy-game.

Intimacy in Its Sexual Dimension

The magnitude of the language problem is illuminated and compounded by a current world movement—the rebirth of feminism.

CONSCIOUSNESS AND THE ULTIMATE

> **Ms.**
> Long-pent,
> the fair princess
> escaped from her bower,
> tired of life in an ovary
> tower.[20]

In her escape from the stereotype constructed for her by societies dominated by males ever since the nomads with their sky gods swooped down and took over the farming villages and their earth goddesses, one of modern woman's targets has been the language of religion. Admitting that religious thinkers are forced to depend heavily upon the use of symbol, metaphor, and analogy to try to describe the indescribable, emancipated woman nevertheless forcefully points out the impact of masculine God-language.

Inevitably, when words like "father" and "king" are used to evoke the image of a personal God, at some level of consciousness it is a male image that takes hold. And since the same words are used in reference to male human beings—from whom, out of the need for analogy, the images of God have been drawn—female human beings are perceived as less godlike, less perfect, different, "the other."[21]

Rita Gross maintains that the inability to say God-She is the ultimate symbol of feminine degradation, since in world perspective, God-She is more common than God-He, and especially since God-She appears, in an irrepressible tendency, even in male-dominant systems (Yahweh as midwife and seamstress, Jesus as feminist, and Virgin Mary as deity). She calls first for a replacement of masculine images with androgenous ones; second, for an emerging feminine image that includes as many nonmaternal as maternal features, and elements of power and transcendence, as well; and third, for a reconciliation of opposites.[22]

The blurring of sexual boundaries between us and them is yet another recurrence of the theme. This call for a specifically sexual intimacy through the breakdown of rigid, repressive stereotypes is at the level of God-talk, as well as at the level of, and inseparable from, interpersonal relationships.

STAGE SIX: INTIMACY
Intimacy in Its Theological Dimension

At first there was stunned silence in hallowed theological halls as the last angry shout of radical theologian Altizer's announcement of the death of God echoed. But quickly, equally angry opposition came forth in rebuttal. Bumper stickers appeared with the slogan, "I know God lives; I spoke to Him this morning!" The death-of-God movement was decried as a sensational absurdity.

Even Cox's more moderate position—that God is immanent within the secular city; that his kingdom is equivalent to the secularization process and that we should look for God there, where the action is—was criticized on the ground that the God of the biblical revelation cannot be equated with everything that goes on in decadent modern society.

A revival of transcendence began. The theology of hope (Moltmann) and eschatological theology (Pannenberg) offered a corrective to the immanentism of radical theology: God is transcendent in that he comes to us from the future; not to be found in the present, God is on the horizon. Therefore the Christian always must be concerned with trying to effect the best changes and, in this view, essentially becomes a revolutionary. Yet critics were not comfortable with the polite curse on the present that was being called down by the theology of hope.[23]

At approximately the same time the theology of hope was becoming popular (late 1960s), yet another approach emerged—process theology. Springing from the philosophical thought of A. N. Whitehead, the process theology of Cobb, Wieman, Williams, Pittenger, and others, blends the best elements of radical theology's immanentism and eschatological theology's transcendence.

In this theology God is immanent within the evolutionary process, but he transcends it, both in the sense of pulling it forward toward himself and in the sense that he is himself personal or the hyper-personal. Here human self-transcendence may serve as an analogy, though by no means a perfect one. I am totally within my physical body. You may see all of me. And yet, as a person, I am more than that. I can interact with myself, I can form a community

CONSCIOUSNESS AND THE ULTIMATE

with others. I am free to interact with and to control nature. By analogy God relates to his creation in this way. He is within all and through all and yet above all.[24]

In process theology, then, Jesus Christ is the classic, specific instance of what God is always doing generally; he includes (not excludes) all that is truly human; he defines (not confines) the ceaseless working of God for us humans and for our salvation; his free, full, and obedient human response to the divine loving invitation establishes the potential loveliness of all humans.[25] The resurrected Christ is loose, potential in every moment as the Holy Spirit, to enable free creaturely response.

Summary: A Typology of the Intimacy Stage

In the developing religious consciousness, the clear-cut boundaries of the medieval synthesis between us and them, sacred and secular, God and man, and saved and lost, were increasingly eroded by the secularization process. This adolescent expression of Western religious development has been impinged upon by an atom bomb, which induced a now nearly complete dissolving of those boundaries in an intimate, irreversible intermingling of us/them, sacred/secular, God/human, saved/lost categories symbolized in the resurrected, loosed Christ, potential in every life situation, as expressed through the symbol of the Holy Spirit and as experienced in the demographic, ecological, economic, political, philosophical, sexual, and theological dimensions of life.

CHAPTER 8

STAGE SEVEN: GENERATIVITY

The Specific Hypothesis

Before adolescent secularization has run its full course—even before young-adult issues of the meaning of intimacy have had time to be clearly focused—humankind, its religiousness now almost thoroughly loosed from its bonds and permeating all life's dimensions in a way reminiscent of the so-called primitive world-view, faces a choice between two radically different pictures of the future.

One vision is idyllic. Containing and realizing the fondest dreams of human beings down through the ages, this heavenly picture of the postsecular age portrays Spaceship Earth on course, each of its crew imbued with a sense that crew membership is, in itself, a precious gift—an honor freely bestowed by an inexpressible, dependable Mystery.

Furthermore, each of the crew, dedicated to responsible crew membership as the actualizing of his or her creative potential as present in each moment, consciously would seek to treat each of the other members as he himself or she herself would wish to be treated. Each would work toward maintenance of responsible crew leadership and governance and would seek to maintain crew size at an optimal level of comfort for all its members, with equitable access to the ship's resources, opportunities, and justice.

The crew of Spaceship Earth would have learned well the lessons of their religious history. They would recognize the religious impulse as a universal, humanizing quality, having to do with one's sense of beginnings and endings, of belonging, of uniqueness, of purposiveness; of relating to one's inner self, to others, and to the environment. All this would be permeated with a sense of awe and mystery, born of the insight that the more one knows, the less one knows.

The members would be constantly on guard against the temptation to objectify expressions of the universal religious impulse (that perhaps most subjective of all human qualities), thereby demonstrating their mastery of the most profound religious lesson of all. They would keep before them the words of Karl Barth.

At the moment when religion becomes conscious of religion, when it becomes a psychologically and historically conceivable magnitude in the world, it falls away from its inner character, from its truth, to idols. Its truth is its otherworldliness, its refusal of the idea of sacredness, its non-historicity.[1]

This zenith of human achievement of maximal creative potential is analogous to the best possible resolution of the individual development crisis, characterized by Erikson as the middle-adulthood attempt at generativity: the literal generation and nurture of children; the picking up and carrying of societal responsibilities in its institutional life; the creative expression of full adult potential. The religious doctrine in focus at the feeling level in individuals who have reached middle adulthood is the doctrine of Creation.[2]

Using an ever-increasing mastery over the stuff of the universe—matter—humans in this heavenly vision would respectfully create and control life itself in its many forms. Perhaps the ultimate fantasy-trip involves the eventual ability of the mind to free itself from matter, literally releasing the human psyche or spirit from its mortal bonds, in attainment of eternal life.

Teilhard de Chardin, Scientist/Philosopher/ Theologian of the Creative Future

Pierre Teilhard was born in 1881 in Auvergne, France, the fourth of eleven children of an amateur natural historian. As

STAGE SEVEN: GENERATIVITY

a boarder in a Jesuit school from the age of ten, he did well in his studies and became especially interested in geology. At eighteen, he entered the Jesuit order and was ordained a priest in 1912. By then he was an accomplished paleontologist as well as a student of Bergson's works on evolution.

After service in World War I as a stretcher-bearer, he took vows of poverty, chastity, and obedience in 1918, and he worked professionally as a paleontologist. Philosophically, he sought to build a general theory of evolution with implications for the future, incorporating human history as well as biology; theologically, he sought to reconcile his evolutionary theory with his Christian faith. After years of travail, brought about primarily by the conflict between his sense of mission for his task and his commitment to obey superiors who saw his ideas as unorthodox, if not heretical, he achieved in large measure the goals he sought.[3]

Teilhard's most important work, *The Phenomenon of Man*, explains his theory of the processes of evolution. Detached from the sun's surface some thousands of millions of years ago in the course of astral evolution, a fragment of matter began to roll itself up—to condense—into the planet Earth. From the lifeless layer of inorganic matter which Teilhard calls the lithosphere, after an immense duration of time, a living layer—the biosphere—evolved. After countless more centuries had passed, a morphologically slight, but incredibly significant, leap occurred. Prehumans became human with the birth of thought, thereby heralding the beginning of a third, thinking layer, named by Teilhard the noosphere. At this point in the story, what had been a biological uphill drive against the forces of entropy became primarily a psychosocial process—one that continues today, toward what he calls megasynthesis.

And now, as a germination of planetary dimensions, comes the thinking layer which over its full extent develops and intertwines its fibres, not to confuse and neutralise them but to reinforce them in the living unity of a single tissue.

Really I can see no coherent, and therefore scientific, way of grouping this immense succession of facts but as a gigantic psycho-biological operation, a sort of *megasynthesis*, the 'super-arrangement' to which all thinking elements of the earth find themselves today individually and collectively subject.

The outcome of the world, the gates of the future, the entry into the super-human—these are not thrown open to a few of the privileged nor to one chosen people to the exclusion of all others. They will open only to an advance of *all together*, in a direction in which *all together* can join and find completion in a spiritual renovation of the earth.[4]

The image that Teilhard selected to describe the final synthesis—the convergence of the noosphere, the centering of the universal and personal in what he terms the "hyper-personal"—is the Omega Point. This final state would not be a fusion of many thinking elements in a loss of identity (a pantheistic dissolving of drops in an ocean of the All). On the contrary, the closer each element of consciousness were to the others, the more it would become itself and the more distinct from the others it would be. "Union differentiates."[5]

From the present, minds are destined to move toward Mind along three discernible lines of advance: the organization of research, as humanity consolidates its efforts to penetrate—intellectually unify and harness—the surrounding energies; the concentration of that research upon human beings, especially in the care and improvement of the body, with attention to the medical and moral factors that should replace crude, haphazard forces of natural selection; and the conjunction of science and religion, in the sense that it is the same life that animates both—that each is a phase of the same complete act of knowledge.[6]

Is this thrust toward fulfillment at the Omega Point inevitable? These words from the heart of the text seem to focus Teilhard's deepest sense of the future.

Once and once only in the course of its planetary existence has the earth been able to envelop itself with life. Similarly once and once only has life succeeded in crossing the threshold of reflection. For thought, as for life, there has been just one season. And we must not forget that since the birth of thought man has been the leading shoot of the tree of life. That being so, the hopes for the future of the noosphere (that is to say, of biogenesis, which in the end is the same as cosmogenesis) are concentrated exclusively upon him as

STAGE SEVEN: GENERATIVITY

such. How then could he come to an end before his time, or stop, or deteriorate, unless the universe committed abortion upon itself, which we have already decided to be absurd?[7]

2001: A Space Odyssey, *As a Mythic Anticipation of the Creative Future*

Re-mythologizing is a seemingly inevitable, legitimate, and vital continuing human effort to express the inexpressible. The science-fiction story, *2001: A Space Odyssey,* is a mythic expression of the creative vision of the future, which accepts the intimate phenomenon of the blurring boundaries between us and them discussed in the previous chapter, and which dramatizes Teilhard's thrust toward fulfillment at the Omega Point.

Joseph Campbell holds that a living myth first must contain the mystical: It must somehow waken and maintain a sense of awe, humility, and respect. Second, it should render a believable image of the universe—that is, a cosmology. Third, it is necessary that it validate and maintain an established moral and social order. And fourth, a living mythology must provide a psychological centering, a harmonizing of the individual.[8]

2001: A Space Odyssey, originally a screenplay and M.G.M. film by Stanley Kubrick and Arthur C. Clarke, later released in book form, begins some hundred thousand years before the four great ice ages and toward the end of a ten-million-year drought on the African equator (Garden of Eden?).[9] Moon-Watcher (Adam?), his women and children, and the others in a little tribal band living in adjacent hillside caves, were near starvation, unaware of the potential source of nourishment in the herds of animals that surrounded them, competing for berries, roots, and leaves.

Suddenly from the sky dropped a rectangular crystal slab, which somehow interacted with Moon-Watcher and his group via hypnosis and a process not clearly described, but seeming somewhat like possession. This intervention, after a period of evaluative probing, resulted in the stimulation of new skills—knot-tying and the use of stones as weapons (tree of knowledge of good and evil?). After waiting to be assured that the intervention would ensure Moon-Watcher's survival, as vividly dramatized by the slaying of a leopard (the Devil?) and a rival chief (Abel?), the block departed (exit from the Garden, from God's presence?).

The next scene opens at the beginning of the twenty-first century A.D., in a Florida space port, where Dr. Heywood Floyd (John the Baptist?) is embarking on a special mission to the moon on behalf of the United States (chosen people?), to examine a black crystalline slab, measuring ten by five feet (burning bush, pillar of fire, etc.?). This slab had been buried thirty feet below the moon's surface and was discovered during a routine magnetic survey. Labeled TMA-1 (for tycho monolith), it had been dug around and studied. At the lunar dawn, with Dr. Floyd present, it suddenly releases "a piercing electronic shriek," followed by four more. Floyd and his associates conclude that this device is a sentinel, planted three million years earlier by a superior extraterrestial intelligence to signal humanity's increasing technological competence.

Disguising the real intent of its mission in order to avoid earthwide panic, the space ship Discoverer is sent toward Saturn's eighth moon, Japetus, the target of the impulses released by TMA-1. First Captain David Bowman (Jesus Christ?); Frank Poole (Simon Peter?), his associate; three hibernating scientists; and a computer named HAL (short for Heuristically Programmed Algorithmic Computer 9000), are the passengers.

HAL (the Devil?), torn by the conflict between truth and his orders to conceal the nature of the mission from Bowman and Poole, seeks to destroy them and take over the mission. He is almost successful. Of the five-man crew, only Bowman survives the eerie struggle, triumphing at last over the robot's evil presence (temptations in the wilderness?).

At last armed with information about the true nature of the mission, Bowman orbits Japetus, only to find on its surface a mile-high slab with the same proportions as those of TMA-1—1:4:9. Flying over it in a space pod, Bowman somehow is drawn into the top as it becomes a duct—a star gate—through which his pod hurtles, finally faster than the speed of light, into a reverse world with a softly glowing,

STAGE SEVEN: GENERATIVITY

milky sky above, sprinkled with myriads of tiny black dots—stars!

He drops through another rectangular passage at increasing speeds and realizes he has passed through a cosmic switching device. This time he exits into space as he has known it but, he realizes, far, far from his own solar system. Compelled toward a huge red sun, Bowman feels only mild apprehension; he senses he is "under the protection of some controlling and almost omnipotent intelligence" (the Holy Spirit?).

With a soft bump, the space pod lands within the red sun. To his astonishment Bowman finds himself and his pod inside a luxuriously appointed hotel suite. He is aware that, should this be some sort of test, not only his fate, but that of the entire human race could depend upon his response (theory of atonement?). The furniture seems real enough, but he discovers that the Washington, D.C., telephone book has only blank pages of paperlike material, that drawers do not open, and that there is no dial tone when he picks up the vision-phone receiver. A strange, delicious blue substance fills each food container; distilled water flows from the tap; a bedside television set shows two-year-old programs; a closet is filled with slightly out-of-date, furry-textured suits. Exhausted, Bowman lies down to sleep "for the last time" (crucifixion?).

Only vaguely aware, Bowman's mind is invaded, and he passes into a realm of consciousness never before experienced by humans (third heaven?), where time runs backward as his life and memory unreel with ever-increasing speed. All the way back to childhood he is rushed; then, with a slowing of the process, time seems frozen for a moment. "The timeless instant passed; the pendulum reversed its swing. In an empty room, floating amid the fires of a double star twenty thousand light-years from Earth, a baby opened its eyes and began to cry" [resurrection?].[10]

In a gradually dawning awareness aided by a glimmering rectangle's confident input (process theology?), trembling with anticipation of the eternity ahead (eternal life?), calmed by the awareness that he is at home (the New Jerusalem?) and that he will never again be alone or without help (the Holy Spirit?), "he launched himself across the light-years." Arriving on earth, he triggers its massed defensive atomic weapons almost casually, with only a thought about a preference for a cleaner sky (the Flood?). He is master of the world and confident that he will think of something to do with it!

2001: A Space Odyssey is a living myth in the best sense of Campbell's definition—a profound expression of the creative future.

The mystical is ever-present, grossly objectified in the 1:4:9 blocks and therefore clearly distinct from the subjective intelligence behind them. The interest of that intelligence in the fulfillment of human potential, even to the point of occasional intervention and interaction within the human evolutionay process, inspires a sense of awe, humility, and respect.

The view of the universe depicted in *2001* is an imaginative combination of the known and the unknown, much more believable to moderns than the biblical cosmology of the three-storied universe.

Since *2001* describes the transitional period between life as we know it and life on a higher level—a new form of life—Campbell's third quality for a living myth, that of the validation of an established moral and social order, at first glance seems to be missing. A closer look reveals the validation of at least continued movement toward such an order and therefore comes as close as could be expected of any narrative of transition.

As for the psychological centering and harmonizing of the individual, *2001* centers upon a representative human, David Bowman. He becomes adventurer, explorer, hero, and at last destroyer/savior of all humanity through the sacrificial death/resurrection, overcoming the obstacles along the way to the very best of his ability. This is a model of maximal psychological-centering and minimal intrapsychic disharmony—David Bowman has it all together, and he goes all the way to the goal.

STAGE SEVEN: GENERATIVITY

Summary: A Typology of the Generativity Stage

The image of humanity as the caring, responsible crew of Spaceship Earth dominates the view of the future at its most creative. At that stage, humanity would be on guard against the temptation to reobjectify the inexpressible, dependable Mystery.

The philosophy of Teilhard de Chardin, and *2001: A Space Odyssey* as a living myth, provide a solid basis for the vision of the creative future, in which humanity, reaching toward the fulfillment of its potential, converges upon the Omega Point in a megasynthesis of the universal and the personal in the hyper-personal.

CHAPTER 9

STAGE EIGHT: INTEGRITY

The Specific Hypothesis

The other option for the future is the horrific, demonic, destructive vision, in which humankind wreaks its own violent end via forces unleashed, either accidently or purposively, either consciously or unconsciously (does it matter which?), by its own hand.

This hellish picture of the postsecular age portrays humanity as the proper English schoolboys in William Gerald Golding's *Lord of the Flies*, marooned on island Earth, and minus the eventual rescue. With the increasing stress of trying to stay alive, the boys' civilized veneer peels off, leaving only individual instinctual drives, which lead ever more quickly to the destruction of the group.

This nightmarish nadir of human regression to its most bestial instinctual level and collective self-destruction would be analogous to the worst possible resolution of the last individual developmental crisis. This is characterized by Erikson as the late adulthood unsuccessful attempt to look back with integrity; the inability to say about one's life, "I may have done this or that a little differently, but it has been a basically good, satisfying life." Erikson's word for this feeling of futility is "despair." The religious doctrine in focus at the feeling level for individuals attaining old age is that of eschatology—of last things.[1]

Warring nations and guerilla bands would continue to raise up projections of their self-wills as gods. Worshiping these icons of their own making, whether they be named Yahweh, Allah, God, dialectical materialism, national advantage, revenge, profit, or whatever, humans would sooner or later unleash the atomic, chemical, or biological forces culminating in the destruction of world civilization as we know it.

Jean-Paul Sartre, Novelist/Playwright/ Philosopher of the Destructive Future

Jean-Paul Sartre was born in Paris, France, in 1905. While Sartre was still a baby, his father died of tropical fever and his mother resumed her role as daughter in her own parents' home. Sartre's life as younger brother to his mother/older sister led him to believe that he had been spared an Oedipus complex. However, his fascination with the Electra myth and his claim that incestuous brother-sister relationships were the only ones for which he had any feeling, indicate that he merely may have traded names for the same conflict.

His grandfather, a teacher of German in French schools, dominated the family. He attempted to dedicate Jean-Paul to literature, but Jean-Paul resisted, preferring detective stories. In 1929 he emerged from the Ecole Normale, having failed his finals. He taught for the next ten years, except for one, during which he studied German phenomenology in Berlin.

In the phenomenology of Husserl he found emancipation from what he believed to be the deception built into the French reflective philosophical tradition. Going even beyond Husserl, his first philosophical work, *The Transcendence of the Ego* (1936), disposes of Husserl's "transcendental ego" as a lapse into the very subjective idealism he was trying to surpass. The true enemy for Sartre is not Husserl, however, but self-consciousness, which attempts to transcend experiences by providing them with a predetermined structure, enabling one to seem to be conscious of such experiences as attributes of the self. Actually, he holds, we are what we prefer.

CONSCIOUSNESS AND THE ULTIMATE

Sartre's first novel, *Nausea* (1938), was his spiritual autobiography. Set in "Filthville" (actually Rouen, where he had worked as a teacher), it lifts up the disparity between the phenomenological search for truth anywhere and the absurdly apparent solidity of the real world. Roquentin (Sartre), failing to discover what he "prefers," ends up "preferring" nausea, the most extreme form of anxiety.

As an atheistic existentialist philosopher (existence precedes essence; to hell with "I think"; to hell with "therefore"; I am, therefore it is hell), Sartre provides the philosophical basis for this study's destructive vision of the future. His writings and his person, vividly centering in upon despair, embody the unsuccessful resolution of the final individual developmental crisis depicted by Erikson.

In the play *No Exit* (1944), Sartre dramatizes the very opposite of Teilhard's vision. Rather than a glorious coming together, an Omega Point of heavenly culmination where all thinking elements converge in an ultimate oneness/individuation, Sartre depicts the final convergence of only three persons as the essence of hell.

INEZ: Wait! You'll see how simple it is. Childishly simple. There isn't any physical torture. And yet we're in Hell. And no one else will come here. We'll stay in this room together, the three of us, for ever and ever. In short there's someone missing here, the official torturer.

GARCON: (Sotto voce) I'd noticed that.

INEZ: It's obvious they're economizing on manpower. The same idea as in a cafeteria, where the customers serve themselves.

ESTELLE: What are you getting at?

INEZ: I mean that each of us will act as a torturer for the other two. . . .

(later)

GARCON: You're crazy, both of you. Don't you see where this will end up? Now shut up. (Pause) Let's all of us sit down again quietly, close our eyes. Each of us must try to forget the presence of the others.

(*A pause.* GARCON *sits down. The women are returning hesitantly to their places. Suddenly* INEZ *swings around*)

INEZ: Forget? How silly can you get! I feel you even in my bones. Your silence shrieks in my ears. You can nail up your mouth, cut your tongue out, but how can that keep you from being there? Can you stop thinking? I hear it, ticking away like an alarm clock, and I know you hear me thinking. It's all very well slouching on your sofa, but you are everywhere, and every sound comes to me soiled, because you've intercepted it on its way.[2]

On the Beach, *As a Mythic Anticipation of the Destructive Future*

Even as *2001: A Space Odyssey* dramatizes vividly, in a mythic, optimistic vision of the future, the freeing of humankind from the limits of mass, time, and space, *On the Beach* pictures the antithesis. It is a vivid mythic drama of the pessimistic, destructive vision of the future—the bondage and final self-annihilation of humankind within the contaminated radioactive atmosphere of the earth by a meaningless, horrible accident of war.

The scene is Melbourne, Australia, in the early 1960s (the book was published in 1957). The entire northern hemisphere of the earth has been contaminated with lethal levels of radiation from a thirty-seven-day atomic war triggered by an Albanian atomic bomb dropped on Naples. Someone unknown then bombed Tel Aviv. After a demonstration/warning flight over Cairo by Britain and the United States, the angry Egyptians atom-bombed Washington and London in Russian bombers with Russian markings. The Americans then bombed Russia. China, seeking to take advantage of the situation, cobalt-bombed Russia, receiving the same treatment in return. By this time the war was being conducted by very junior officers using extensive stockpiles of bombs and aircraft; it continued until those reserves were depleted, and the atmosphere was thoroughly poisoned.

As the narrative begins, the radioactive materials in the atmosphere are gradually creeping southward, knocking out city after city in their wake as their entire populations become ill and die of radiation sickness. Lieutenant Commander Peter Holmes of the Royal Australian Navy, a

CONSCIOUSNESS AND THE ULTIMATE

young husband and father, is assigned as liaison officer to U.S.S. Scorpion, an American atomic-powered submarine and the only long-range vessel still operational. Commander Dwight Towers is in command.

Towers is ordered to travel submerged into the danger zone to investigate a mysterious, sporadic signal transmitted from the vicinity of Seattle, Washington. Since this is the sole communications activity in the northern hemisphere, it offers a note of hope. Also, one scientist has advanced the theory that the contamination levels should now be dissipating to livable tolerances in the far north, a second thread of hope that the mission seeks to investigate.

Making its way northward, the Scorpion arrives in Puget Sound, having traced the radio signal backward to its source—a naval communications-school transmitter on Santa Maria Island. A lieutenant familiar with the area is sent ashore in protective suit with oxygen supply, to find the mystery telegrapher.

He went upstairs, and found the main transmitting room. There were two transmitting desks, each with a towering metal frame of grey radio equipment in front of it. One of these sets was dead and silent, the instruments all at zero.

The other set stood by the window, and here the casement had been blown from its hinges and lay across the desk. One end of the window frame projected outside the building and teetered gently in the light breeze. One of the upper corners rested on an overturned Coke bottle on the desk. The transmitting key lay underneath the frame that rested unstably above it, teetering a little in the wind. He reached out and touched it with his gloved hand. The frame rocked on the transmitting key, and the needle of a milliammeter upon the set flipped upwards. He released the frame, and the needle fell back.[3]

Later, the U.S.S. Scorpion inches its way up the Gulf of Alaska, using its underwater mine detector to signal the presence of icebergs. Near Kodiak, at latitude 58° north, in nearly impassable ice, they find the radiation level just as lethal as ever. Missions accomplished. Both tenuous hopes are without logical bases. The travelers return to Australia, to spend the remaining weeks of life as best they can.

STAGE EIGHT: INTEGRITY

Peter Holmes busies himself in domestic activity with his wife and daughter at his cottage near Melbourne. On his last day of life he travels to town to bring back a garden seat for his wife. That evening, just before taking cyanide pills to avoid the final agonies of radiation sickness, the Holmes talk.

Presently she said, "Peter, why did all this happen to us? Was it because Russia and China started fighting each other?"

He nodded. "That's about the size of it," he said. "But there was more to it than that. America and England and Russia started bombing for destruction first. The whole thing started with Albania."

"But we didn't have anything to do with it at all, did we—here in Australia?"

"We gave England moral support," he told her. "I don't think we had time to give her any other kind. The whole thing was over in a month."

"Couldn't anyone have stopped it?"

"I don't know. . . . Some kinds of silliness you just can't stop," he said. "I mean, if a couple of hundred million people all decide that their national honour requires them to drop cobalt bombs upon their neighbor, well, there's not much that you or I can do about it. The only possible hope would have been to educate them out of their silliness."[4]

Doing his duty until the very last, Dwight Towers sails the Scorpion out to sea to be scuttled, lest her unguarded secrets fall into a nonexistent enemy's hands.

Here, as in the case of *2001: A Space Odyssey*, are all the qualities defined by Campbell as necessary for a living myth. The eerie, invisible, gradual, but inevitable approach of the radiation-polluted air is the central theme and driving force behind the narrative. It is almost as if the Devil himself is rolling out a malevolent blanket of death. Yet the Devil evaporates as the situation is explained scientifically and politically, leaving only the minor demons of absurd accident and blind pride to take the blame, if projections and personifications must be created to account for the disaster.

CONSCIOUSNESS AND THE ULTIMATE

The view of the cosmos depicted in *On the Beach* is only too real—only too believable to the modern mind. Dependable natural laws govern throughout—split an atom, release tremendous power; pollute the atmosphere with radioactive materials, die of radiation sickness.

In addition, *On the Beach* grimly validates by negation the prevailing established moral and social order. It is the precarious order founded upon *lex talionis,* which crumbles in the final, accidently triggered, and reflexively fought holocaust.

Finally, *On the Beach* describes the ultimate psychological destruction of all human beings, along with the destruction of every other aspect of life. It should be noted that some of the horror is removed from this final psychological disintegration through death, because characters in the story find a certain integrity in their attempts to cope with impending doom. Peter Holmes finds loyalty to his wife and child at the center of his being and chooses to die with them. Dwight Towers, though separated from his wife and children by their death, fantasizes going home even to the end, while guiding his ship toward its final resting place. Duty seems to be his centering point. But disintegration of mind/body is the inevitable outcome for all the characters in the book, as well as for all humankind.

Summary: A Typology of the Integrity Stage

The image of humanity as narrowly nationalistic, victim of the absurdly accidental release of destructive power by human hands upon human heads, with the resultant total destruction, dominates the view of the future at its most despairing—at the moment of humanity's horrible eschatological last gasp. Humanity at this stage would be dragged down to its genocide in a final triumph of the forces of evil—of meaningless, chance absurdity—over whatever remains of the good, the purposive, the hopeful.

The atheistic existentialism of Jean-Paul Sartre offers the philosophical basis, and *On the Beach* demonstrates the living, mythic vision of a destructive future.[5]

# PART II

PSYCHOLOGY:
THE ONTOGENY OF CONSCIOUSNESS OF THE ULTIMATE

CHAPTER 10

THE PSYCHOLOGY OF RELIGION

From Phylogeny to Ontogeny

The ongoing story of humanity's rising consciousness of the ultimate, reduced to Eriksonian categories (phylogeny), has led from the dawn of history to two startlingly opposed projections for the future. The question immediately arises, Can the future be shaped in such a way as to help bring about the creative vision and avoid the destructive one? And on its heels come the companion questions. Do persons today, given the current levels of religious consciousness, have the resources to so influence the future? And, What is the present status of that religious consciousness?

Answers to such global questions must be sought in a consideration of the state of development of individual religious sensitivities and capabilities (ontogeny) as studied and understood in today's world. The discipline ostensibly undertaking that task is the psychology of religion.

Early Philosophical Threads

The indirect philosophical threads of the psychology of religion can be traced back at least as far as Socrates (469–399 B.C.) and his emphasis on the human inner nature. Plato (429–347 B.C.) first hinted at an unconscious entity within the human, as he developed his philosophy of knowledge derived from universal ideas and from his concept of the eternal psyche. Experience as a source of knowledge entered the picture in the thinking of Aristotle (384–322 B.C.). Augustine of Hippo (A.D. 354–430) added an internal sense whereby humans can arrive at knowledge of God.

Scholasticism contributed to the developing understanding of the soul-mind and its functioning, with Anselm (1034–1109), who maintained that faith is derived from emotion, experiences, and will, as well as from Scriptures and dogma; with Thomas Aquinas (1224–1275), who saw in the human a uniting of the realms of matter and form, with form including soul as spiritual principle; with Duns Scotus (1264–1308) and his emphasis on will; with Meister Eckhart (1260–1327) and his lifting up of the mystical, vis-á-vis the rational.

René Descartes (1596–1650) saw mind and body as separate substances, with mind a "thinking thing"—that which thinks always. John Locke (1632–1704) disagreed, saying that the mind thinks only when a person is conscious of such activity; that initially the mind is a *tabula rasa*. Liebnitz (1646–1716) agreed with Descartes and reasoned toward unconscious thinking via his doctrine of petite perceptions. Kant (1724–1804) went beyond petite perceptions to what he termed "non-conscious processes."

Schopenhauer (1788–1860) provided the last stepping-stone toward full conceptualization of the unconscious with his contribution that the will controls the emergence of ideas into and their disappearance out of consciousness; F.W.H. Myers (1843–1901) used Schopenhauer's idea to arrive at his concept of a subliminal, or ultramarginal self, an essential ingredient in the philosophical basis for the psychology of religion.[1]

The New Science Versus Western Christian Theology

In the late nineteenth and early twentieth centuries, at least three science-related yet disparate forces combined to challenge Western Christian theology. The first force was the evolutionary theory of Charles Darwin (1809–1882) set forth in *The Origin of Species*, which had the effect of polarizing scientific data about the age of the earth and about the ways the species came into being, as opposed to those who maintained a literal interpretation of all Scripture and upheld a constant level of verbally inspired authorship of the entire Bible.

The second force in the polarization was the biblical and higher criticism that was developed to its fullest refinement by German Old Testament scholars, and which applied scientifically based techniques to an analysis of the texts and forms of Scripture, to hypothesize, for example, at least four separate strands of authorship within the book of Genesis alone (JEDP theory). Julius Wellhausen (1844–1918) popularized this movement with his book *Prolegomena to the History of Israel*.

The third force was Sigmund Freud (1856–1939), though the impact of his theories of sexuality, psychosexual development, and religion as a massive projection of the wish for a kindly father, initially was felt primarily only in the United States. It was Freud who, through his innovative, even agonizing work to elaborate and practice doctrines of psychoanalysis, provided an essential ingredient for the psychology of religion.[2]

The Emergence of the Psychology of Religion

In the no-man's-land between the two warring camps, there were those who refused to accept as final the claim that the new science and Western Christian theology must remain forever enemies. One of these persons, G. Stanley Hall, the first doctor of philosophy in psychology in the United States and president of Clark University, published an article in the *Princeton Review* in 1882, entitled "The Moral and Religious Training of Children," in which he emphasized the implications for religious education that might lie in the changes in the minds and bodies of early adolescents. This was the first of several significant published efforts of the Clark School. The emergence of psychology of religion as a legitimate area of study was underway.

CONSCIOUSNESS AND THE ULTIMATE

According to James Bissett Pratt, the first article of great intrinsic value came out of Clark University in 1896 and was authored by James H. Leuba.[3] It was a study from published accounts of conversion, titled "The Psychology of Religious Phenomena." Then in 1903, a now classic study by yet another member of the Clark School, based on results of eight hundred questionnaires regarding conversion experiences, was published by Edwin D. Starbuck under the title *The Psychology of Religion*. He concluded in this earliest quantitative research effort that conversions and puberty tend to supplement each other in time, rather than coincide, but that they may be mutually conditioned.[4]

Shortly before Starbuck's work came out, William James delivered the 1901–1902 Gifford Lectures at Edinburgh, in which he shared insights from an empirical study of biographies, concluding, among other things, that a religious view of the universe is nearer the truth than a limited view based on natural science. This effort, published as *The Varieties of Religious Experience*, is recognized by Pratt as the most important single contribution of those early days.[5]

From those beginnings has evolved an extensive literature and variously described subgroupings of the psychologists of religion. In his article "A Critical Survey of the Psychology of Religion," Hopkins identifies six classifications—six schools—and their proponents.[6]

1. The "rational-naturalistic school" is exemplified in the approach of J. G. Frazer in *The Golden Bough*; here the impact of animism, as well as philosophical arguments for purpose in the world, as derived logically from observed orderliness, are emphasized.
2. The "sociological school," which relates the rise of creeds to the class struggle, is best illustrated in Karl Marx and *Das Kapital*.
3. The "anthropological school" brings a distinct anthropological interpretation of religion from its study of the races and cultures of mankind, as in J. D. Unwin's *Sex and Culture*.

4. The "classical psychological school" is Hopkins' label for the grouping that includes such fathers as Starbuck and James.
5. The "libidinal school," stressing religious emblems as phallic symbols, is the category developed by Freud and elaborated in *Totem and Taboo*.
6. The "eclectic school," as the name implies, draws on all the other schools and is represented by Ernest Ligon's *The Psychology of Christian Personality*.

Hiltner isolates five "streams" within the discipline of psychology of religion.[7]

1. The "main stream" repeats the pioneers' approach and methodology.
2. The "philosophical stream" is that in which psychologists of religion developed an apologetic rationale for their work.
3. The "normative, or educational, stream"—the religious education movement—typifies the thinking of Dewey.
4. The "natural science stream" uplifts use of the so-called scientific method.
5. The "therapeutic, or dynamic, stream," focuses upon psychoanalytic theory and the accompanying implications for religion.

The Contribution of Anton Boisen

Anton D. Boisen, the first of two siblings and the only son, was born in 1876 to an Indiana University professor of languages and his gently persuasive wife. Boisen's father died of a heart attack when Anton was seven. He later wrote, "My father thus died when I was only three months past my seventh birthday, but his memory, reinforced by my mother's picture of him and that of others who knew him, has remained a potent force in my life, one which for me has been associated with my idea of God."[8]

Similarly, he wrote that his mother "was gentle and retiring. Throughout her dealings with me she relied on persuasion rather than compulsion. She made me feel bad when I did not do as I ought."[9]

Surrounded by females after his father's death, Boisen emerged as a brilliant but painfully shy young man, suffering briefly from an acute anxiety state. Vocationally, he moved from forester, to seminarian, to rural Midwest and Maine pastor, to World War I worker overseas with the YMCA, and back to the Midwest as a rural survey director.

At this point a largely fantasized love affair and the accompanying feelings of anxiety precipitated his admission, in an acutely psychotic condition, to a psychopathic hospital and then to a state mental hospital. Boisen emerged from a fifteen-month hospitalization strongly believing that the religious dimension plays a vital role in the inner struggle between illness and health; that a sensitive pastor could have been extremely helpful to him during his struggle; and that the careful study of persons in such crises would be useful in the understanding of religion in general and of pastoral care in particular.

After additional study at Harvard and Andover, he became chaplain at Worcester State Hospital in Massachusetts. There he borrowed the newly developed case-study method from Richard C. Cabot and medicine, and applied it to one of the earliest expressions of a now extensive and increasingly accepted experiential adjunct to theological education, known as clinical pastoral education. In the summer of 1925, four theological students studied with what Boisen called living human documents; thus he pioneered in the area between lofty theological academia and hurting human beings, to study along with his students and learn from the patient-parishioners themselves.

A critical technique, the written verbatim record of what transpires between pastor and patient-parishioner, became the vehicle of learning through which the seminarian and/or pastor focuses on the concerns of the one being helped. Also, from what Hall calls Boisen's "tireless empirical study" came his three principal books, *Out of the Depths, Exploration of the Inner World,* and *Religion in Crisis and Custom.*

Boisen's contribution to the psychology of religion was the introduction of firsthand study of the religious dimension in persons, through verbatims and case seminars, at a deeper level than either of the previous methods—the questionnaire of Starbuck, or the approach of James through the review of biographical materials. "Boisen continues to goad the religious community into examination of unusual experiences and into scrutiny of the philosophical presuppositions and value systems of the psychiatric community."[10]

The Crisis in the Psychology of Religion

The person and work of Anton Boisen served to stand as a transition in the crisis that nearly destroyed the psychology of religion as a relevant inquiry for both theologians and psychologists. In a perceptive analysis of the forces precipitating the crisis, Peter Homans describes the realities that evaporated the ideological synthesis at the time of the First World War—theological existentialism, psychoanalysis, and behaviorism.[11]

Before elaborating on these three movements, a word should be said in description, if not in caricature, of the condition of the dominant classical school (Hopkins' term), or main stream (Hiltner's term), of the psychology of religion in 1918. Both James and Hall brought a broadly functional-adaptive psychological point of view to bear upon their work. They saw their task as the description and analysis of the so-called religious referent in terms of both psychic and social adaption: The religious experience, especially the conversion experience, occurs at a particular point in time and is simply and objectively described and analyzed on that basis.

First, theological existentialism, as expressed by Barth, Brunner, Bultmann, Tillich, Reinhold Niebuhr, and H. N. Wieman, rejects religious experience in favor of theological existence, in reaction against the pietistic-moralistic ethos with which classical psychologists of religion had become fatally linked.[12]

Second, psychoanalysis dealt a death blow to classic, or main stream, psychology of religion when Freud assigned religious experience to the level of the repressed or dynamic unconscious, thereby eliminating it as a factor in any normative understanding of psychic life. Further, Freud, in treatment of his patients, attempted to help release them from the binding power of the harsh superego so closely identified with religious expressions following the conversion experience.

Third, Watson's behaviorism attacked the James-Hall approach with a methodology that renders irrelevant the subjective or psychic (and thereby the possibility of religious experience) by permanently dissociating subject and object. Watson considered consciousness and introspection as pseudoproblems preventing meaningful progress in the development of psychology.[13]

Thus Boisen came along at a critical time and provided a bridge between the classical psychologists of religion (James, Hall, Starbuck, *et al.*), and the rising group (Wise, Hiltner, Oates, Johnson, *et al.*), labeled by Homans the pastoral psychologists—exponents of what Hiltner called the therapeutic, or dynamic, stream in the psychology of religion.[14]

Building on the insights of Boisen, this new school has managed an uneasy synthesis on the boundaries between theology and psychology, in which the pastoral counseling process replaces the conversion experience as the central matter of study.

CHAPTER 11

THE FOUR FUNCTIONS OF THE MIND

Beyond the Psychology of Religion

The replacement of the conversion experience by the pastoral counseling process as the central matter of study in the psychology of religion is not sufficient, in itself, to provide more adequate categories for a full appreciation of individual differences in consciousness of the ultimate. The focus remains on feeling, at the expense of the sensation, thinking, or intuitive aspects of human mental functioning today.

Even the most outstanding recent studies reflect this imbalance. Psychologist Paul W. Pruyser places strong emphasis upon perceptual (sensation), intellectual (thinking), and emotional (feeling) processes, but omits intuition altogether.[1] Theologian Wayne E. Oates, on the other hand, lifts up the intuitive in chapters on mysticism and dreams. Feeling gets its due in his overview of the contributions of psychotherapists, and psychologists of personality. Sensation's significance is seen in discussions of ritual and ecstasy. But it seems that the closest he comes to "thinking" as a way toward consciousness of the ultimate is in comments on decision-making.[2]

A balanced set of categories that does not either directly or indirectly give credence to one mind function at the expense of another in individual consciousness of the ultimate, is yet to be found in the psychology of religion. Therefore the theoretical framework for this study is borrowed not from the psychology of religion, but from the analytical psychology of Carl G. Jung.

The Contribution of Carl G. Jung

Carl Gustav Jung was born in 1875 at Kassuyl, Thurgovil, Switzerland, the son of a country parson. Carl's sister was born nine years later. He emerged from boyhood struggles with church and school, decided to study medicine, and received his medical degree from the University of Basel in 1902. During his service as physician to the psychiatric clinic at the University of Zurich, he became a disciple of Freud.

Within a few years, Jung was president of the International Psychoanalytic Society, editor of the *Annual for Psychoanalytical and Psychopathological Research,* and heir apparent to leadership of the entire psychoanalytic movement. His abandonment of certain basic Freudian doctrines and his 1911 split with Freud led him to found his own school of psychology in Zurich. In 1932 he became professor of psychology at the Federal Polytechnical University there, writing and lecturing until his death in 1961.

Jung's collected works comprise twenty thick volumes, each filled with a wandering, overwhelming erudition. Woven into that complex tapestry are his major contributions: archetypes; the collective unconscious; a male and female principle in each sex; introvert/extrovert; the will to wholeness; a self that transcends but does not exclude the ego; a legitimate religious dynamic; and four distinct, yet independent, functions of the psyche.[3] This last concept—the four functions of the psyche (mind)—is the theoretical base upon which is built this study's considerations of contemporary humanity's consciousness of the ultimate.

The Four Functions Defined

1. *Sensation* is defined by Jung as that psychological function which "transmits physical stimulus to perception . . . via the sense organs and 'bodily senses' (kinesthetic, vasomotor sensations, etc.)."[4] Though sensation transmits physical changes to consciousness and therefore represents

THE FOUR FUNCTIONS OF THE MIND

the physiological impulse, it is not identical with it, since it is a merely perceptive function. All this Jung considers sensuous, or concrete, sensation; there is also abstract sensation. Separated from other psychological functions, following its own principle, detached from the admixture of differences of the perceived object and from the subjective admixture of feeling and thought, abstract sensation is pure, artistic, aesthetic.

In relation to the other three functions, Jung sees sensation as an elementary phenomenon, absolutely given, prominent in both the child and the primitive—an irrational function that always predominates over thinking and feeling. Sensation and intuition are a pair of mutually compensating opposites. Jung regards sensation as conscious perception; intuition, as unconscious perception. Thinking and feeling have their origins in sensation.

2. *Feeling* is a rational process that takes place between the ego and a given content, imparting to that process a definite value in the sense of acceptance (like) or rejection (dislike). It can also appear apart from the contents of consciousness or momentary sensations in the form of mood. Such mood may be causally related to either conscious or unconscious contents; in either event it signifies a valuation of the whole consciousness situation of the moment. Feeling is, therefore, an entirely subjective process, which may be completely independent of external stimuli, although "chiming in" with every sensation. Yet it is also a kind of judging, though different from intellectual judging in that it is solely concerned with setting up a subjective criterion of acceptance or rejection. This judgment by feeling extends to every content of consciousness.

Jung distinguishes abstract feeling from ordinary concrete feeling. Abstract feeling, raised above the differences of individual feeling-values, establishes an overall mood or state of feeling. The more abstract a feeling is, the more general and objective is the value it bestows; the more concrete, the more subjective and personal the bestowed value.

Feeling is a rational function, as is thinking, because values in general are bestowed according to the laws of reason. Active feeling is a directed function—an act of will (example: loving). Passive feeling is undirected (example: being in love). When a person's overall attitude is oriented by the feeling function, Jung sees that person as a "feeling type."[5]

3. *Thinking* is an apperceptive, rational activity, which brings given presentations into conceptual connection. Active thought is an act of will, a deliberate act of judgment; passive thinking is an occurrence wherein conceptual connections establish themselves, and in which the formed judgments even may contradict the aims of active thought.

A simple stringing together of representations, seen by some psychologists as associative thinking, is considered by Jung to be mere presentation, not thinking. He prefers to confine thinking to the linking of representations by means of a concept within which an act of judgment prevails.

Though active, directed thinking is a rational function, undirected, passive thinking can be said to be irrational in that it criticizes and arranges representations according to unconscious norms. Also, as already stated, thinking, as well as feeling, has its origins in sensation.

Even as sensation and intuition are a pair of mutually compensating irrational opposites, so thinking and feeling are two rational opposites.[6] Thinking, like feeling, is "directed at something arising in consciousness from within or from without, its goal being to order the perception into some kind of intelligible meaning."[7]

4. *Intuition* is an irrational psychological function "which transmits perceptions in an unconscious way."[8] Both outer and inner objects or their associations—in fact, anything—can be the object of this perception. Though neither sensation, feeling, or intellectual conclusion, intuition is peculiarly able to appear in any one of those three forms. Further, it is a kind of instinctive apprehension, whose contents, like those of sensation, are given, as opposed to derived, as with feeling and thinking.

In its concrete form, intuition carries perceptions concerned with the actuality of things and has a high degree of a participation by sensation. Abstract intuition transmits the perceptions of ideational associations and therefore contains a high degree of participation by thinking.

As with sensation, Jung sees intuition as a characteristic of infantile and primitive psychology and as "the maternal soil from which thinking and feeling are developed in the form of rational functions."[9]

The Four Functions Applied

Each person, according to Jung, differentiates and develops one of the four functions to an extent that it can be said to be the superior, or dominant, function. This process of differentiation is shaped both by predisposition and by conditioning, and its result is that the most differentiated function plays the principal role in one's life.

For example, persons in whom thinking is the most highly differentiated function, will walk into a social gathering and automatically begin to analyze the people within their intellectual frame of reference. The feeling-type person will try to pick up the emotional tenor of the group. The sensation type will be most aware of the look, touch, and smell of the room, while the intuitive will instantly realize the significance and possibilities of the occasion.[10]

In addition, there is a relatively unconscious auxiliary function at work to complement that of the highly differentiated function. Two competing functions cannot work together in this way, however. Feeling can never act secondarily to thinking, because its nature is opposed to thinking. "Thinking, if it is to be real thinking and true to its own principle, must scrupulously exclude feeling."[11] But thinking can readily pair up with either sensation or intuition, the two irrational functions. All this fits, in the Jungian system, into an overall duality of general attitude-types, known as introversion and extroversion, and provides sixteen possible typal combinations. However, at the risk of stripping the Jungian framework of some of its richest meanings, neither the secondary functions nor the general attitude-types will be involved in the schema's use as a basis for the ontogenetic considerations of consciousness of the ultimate.

CONSCIOUSNESS AND THE ULTIMATE

The greatest potential for a more adequate classification of current religious expression lies in the de-emphasis of relative moral valuations within the four functional categories themselves. Jung refuses to lift up thinking as better than (more highly valued than) feeling; or intuition as a greater good than, say, sensation. Apart from a rough sequential division (the irrational functions preceded the rational in the process of evolution), the categories stand as equals.

I have been asked almost reproachfully why I speak of four functions and not of more or fewer. That there are exactly four is a matter of empirical fact. But, as the following consideration will show, a certain completeness is attained by these four. Sensation establishes what is actually given, thinking enables us to recognize its meaning, feeling tells us its value, and finally intuition points to the possibilities of the whence and whither that lie within the immediate facts. . . . The four functions are somewhat like the four points of the compass; they are just as arbitrary and just as indispensable.[12]

CHAPTER 12

SENSATION AND CONSCIOUSNESS OF THE ULTIMATE

The Sensation Typology

Perhaps the most distinct characteristic in persons of the sensation type is primary involvement in the present—an orientation toward the here and now. This temporal existentialism often includes such qualities as seeming disregard of the future, pervasive rejection of the past, spontaneity, unpredictability, high valuation of variety, the tendency to drift, and a sense of the transitory nature of life.

The second characteristic of the sensation type is the affinity for the physical world and an accompanying appreciation of sensual pleasures: the love of good food, good wine, stylish clothes, sexual experiences, a chair before the fire, a cool drink, a comfortable bed, a relaxing massage; the pleasure of tending a garden, mending a fence, cooking a meal. In this type sensuality almost seems to envelop the self. These individuals often exhibit great physical competence, verbal directness, courage, efficiency, and empiricism.

A third sensation-type characteristic is the desire for self-sufficiency. The strong tendency toward trusting only firsthand experience makes it difficult for the sensation type to depend too much upon what someone else does or says. Thus one may tend toward order, precision, directiveness, and the need to control.

In general, sensation types are at their best in crisis situations; prefer life to be a series of peak experiences; tend to view life as a game; often are strong advocates of law and order (because of difficulty in internalizing ethical systems); incorporate the separate moments of their lives via myth, such as heroism in war; and are very susceptible to magic, mystery, and superstition.

Michael Malone lists Mark Antony, Julius Caesar, Geoffrey Chaucer, Henry VIII, Sir Francis Drake, Leo Tolstoy, Benjamin Franklin, Auguste Renoir, Louis Pasteur, Jean Harlow, Gauguin, Ernest Hemingway, Thomas Edison, Babe Ruth, Teddy Roosevelt, Mohandas Gandhi, and Charles Lindbergh, as sensation types.[1]

The Sensation Type, Liturgy, and Good Works

The sensation-dominant person consciously appropriates reality primarily in the present moment, primarily through sensory perceptions of the physical world, and primarily without much reliance on other persons. Furthermore, sensation types who consciously seek the ultimate via forms identified as sacred or religious, find a great affinity for liturgy and/or good works.

Liturgy means "work of the people" and is the active side of religious expression. It is the work of worship.[2] Sensation types in the high-church tradition can literally feast their eyes on the Mass in a vivid atmosphere (windows, walls, statuary, vestments, ornamentation, priestly movements, changing seasonal colors, and special lighting). Other senses are not ignored: There is incense for the olfactory, words and music for the hearing, genuflection for the touch, and Communion for the taste.

Multisensory stimulation abounds in the so-called low-church traditions as well, though noticeably shaped by the various religious attitudes toward sensation itself. Pruyser notes four such attitudes: perceiving as joyously greeted; perceiving as evil, and hence to be minimized; perceiving as both good and evil, requiring selective focus; and perceiving as elevated above routine recognition.[3]

These four attitudes suggest complementary pairings of sensation with the other three functions and their accompanying religious expressions. Sensation as blessing seems

SENSATION

paired with positive feeling and can be seen in nature worship. Sensation as curse represents the other side of the coin—negative feeling—and finds religious expression in asceticism. Sensation as potentially either blessing or curse requires thinking to determine which is which and encompasses the disciplines of systematic theology and ethics. Sensation as springboard to an experience beyond itself involves intuition and finds expression in mysticism.

Physical involvement is not limited to worship in consciousness of the ultimate. In religious life, sensation types find fulfillment in good works and make excellent missionaries, preachers, evangelists, healers, promoters, and controversialists.

Sensation and Natural Literalism: World A

As already noted, Jung sees sensation as an elementary phenomenon, the conscious perception of childhood. Thus, ontogenetically speaking, sensation comes first in consciousness of the ultimate. Direct observation of any infant quickly confirms that sensation is initially the most differentiated mental function. A baby responds directly and unerringly to sense stimulation. Bodily discomfort produces loud cries of protest. A full stomach, warmth, and the mother's loving touch trigger coos of delight. The eyes follow movement and light. Loud noise frightens. Soft music lulls, and so on.

With regard to religious faith, defined by Paul Tillich as the state of being ultimately concerned, childhood is a time of natural literalism. This "primitive period of individuals and groups consists in the inability to separate the creations of symbolic imagination from the facts which can be verified through observation and experiment."[4]

In this childlike state—World A—symbol (that which points beyond itself while participating in that to which it points), the necessary vehicle for expression of ultimate concern, since symbolic language alone is able to express the ultimate, and myth (the combination of symbols of ultimate concern) are understood in their immediate meaning.[5]

CONSCIOUSNESS AND THE ULTIMATE

The material, taken from nature and history, is used in its proper sense. The character of the symbol to point beyond itself to something else is disregarded. Creation is taken as a magic act which happened once upon a time. The fall of Adam is localized on a special geographical point and attributed to a human individual. The virgin birth of the Messiah is understood in biological terms, resurrection and ascension as physical events, the second coming of the Christ as telluric, or cosmic, catastrophe. The presupposition of such literalism is that God is a being, acting in time and space, dwelling in a special place, affecting the course of events and being affected by them like any other being in the universe.[6]

By way of further elaboration, Tillich goes on to say that although the mythical and the literal are indistinguishable in natural literalism, "This stage has a full right of its own and should not be disturbed, either in individuals or in groups, up to the moment when man's questioning mind breaks the natural acceptance of the mythological visions as literal."

Sensation/World A Illuminative Case

A 67-year-old widow from a small community was undergoing surgery for removal of her gall bladder. By grim coincidence, surgeons worked desperately in the very next operating suite to save the life of her 26-year-old grandson, who had been seriously injured when a scaffold had collapsed. They were unsuccessful. The grandson died.

The chaplain recorded some especially significant words from the widow when he visited her the day before the grandson's funeral. She indicated that she had experienced her youngest grandson's drowning 12 years earlier; her husband's death 18 years before; the recent death of her mother, whom she had nursed for almost 50 years; the death of her only son the previous fall; and that of her minister-father when she was 18.

She went on to say, "I guess that I was supposed to go through these things or I would not have had to."

Trying to maintain his own theological system's integrity, the chaplain reacted. "Well, I don't feel that way."

SENSATION

She responded, "Well, the Lord has seen me through, hasn't he? He will see me through this!"

Awed, the chaplain said, "You seem to have a lot of strength."

She went on. "Well, I just live on faith. And I believe that the Lord will see me through." And then, the topper: "I have been through a lot in my life, *and I bet I can go through a lot more!*"

This woman was a World A person. She, in her natural literalism, took her suffering as a matter of course ("I guess that I was supposed to go through these things . . ."). For whatever reasons of capacity and milieu, she remained spiritually preconscious, bearing her burdens completely uncritically. She even became a little huffy when the chaplain seemed unable to accept her nearly absolute serenity in the face of massive accumulated loss ("Well, the Lord has seen me through, hasn't he?").

CHAPTER 13

FEELING AND CONSCIOUSNESS OF THE ULTIMATE

The Feeling Typology

Even as the sensation type is primarily involved in the present, the feeling type centers upon the past. The feeling person tends to attach great significance to both large and small events, all the way back to childhood, continuing to experience them intensely through accurate memory. So cherishing the past, the feeling-dominant type is slow to change, being very reluctant to accept the unfamiliar.

A second major attribute is primacy of the emotions: Great pleasure is received from simple emotional responses. Feeling types often are stirred deeply by strong emotion such as love, hate, fear, lust, joy, and grief, with the accompanying hazard that such feeling, once started, may develop an uncontrollable life of its own. This is a threat to another aspect of the feeling person—the need for emotional unity.

Therefore, in the third vital area—the centrality of relationships—a feeling type would attempt to avoid the acute pain of dissension with a loved one, even to the point of sacrificing a principle. This does not mean, however, that the feeling-differentiated individual is unprincipled. Quite the contrary. In the Jungian scheme, feeling, together with thinking, is a rational, judgmental form of psychic activity, but whereas thinking is objective conceptual connection, feeling is subjective valuation. In the feeling mode, true and false usually translates as right and wrong, like and dislike, good and evil. It is a matter of the heart ruling the head.

Fourth, the feeling person has a strong sense of involvement in the eternal life cycles of humanity and nature. Appreciation for the song of a bird, the sense of reverence for all life, an awareness that primal feelings are a universal bond that join people from every generation in the circle of human existence—these qualities mark the feeling type.

In general, feeling types enjoy stories of the past; are often moody; can delineate and describe feelings accurately; are sensitive to others; find meaning in human relationships; desire to belong; are deeply loyal, romantic, enchanting; tend to worry.

In the feeling category, Malone places St. Francis of Assisi, Blaise Pascal, George Washington, Emily Dickinson, Franz Schubert, Frederick Chopin, William James, Vincent VanGogh, Theodore Dreiser, Robert E. Lee, D. H. Lawrence, Albert Schweitzer, Mao Tse-tung, John Dewey, Dwight Eisenhower, and Pope John XXIII.[1]

The Feeling Type, Pastoral Care, and Glossolalia

The feeling-differentiated person consciously appropriates reality primarily in memories of the past, through emotional responses, and with great value placed on lasting human relationships, all with a sense of harmony within the rhythms of human and natural cycles. Therefore, those feeling types who attempt to appropriate ultimacy through religious forms are especially attracted to pastoral care concerns and/or highly emotion-charged expression, such as glossolalia.

Christian pastoral care has been defined as "the art of communicating the inner meaning of the Gospel to persons at the point of their need."[2] More a function than an activity; more a living relationship than a theory; more a matter of being than of doing, pastoral care is the expression of concern rooted in the Christian belief in the love of God. This primarily Protestant expression, along with its Catholic counterpart, the cure of souls (*cura animarum*), stands in a much wider tradition—spiritual guidance—present in all religions.[3] The definitive features of pastoral care, whatever the forms, whatever the religion, include the attempts of a religious helper to assist a person in need, within a caring (feeling) relationship, which in one way or another acknowledges the presence of the ultimate (God, for some religions).

Glossolalia (literally, *tongue-speaking*) is one example of the discharge of high emotion in a religious setting and is linked to the baptism of the Spirit described in the New Testament book of Acts. Speaking in tongues has found sporadic expression over the centuries and recent acceptance and practice outside the boundaries of the pentecostal churches since 1960.

Best described as unintelligible, ecstatic utterance, tongue-speaking seems most evident in eras that restrain or repress religion, either actively or passively.[4] Why now? Oates holds that today's secular society "represses and selectively ignores religion in reference to God, except as a joke or as profanity." Thus it requires brashness to the point of compulsion to speak openly of God. Psychoanalytically, this nonspeaking taboo has the quality of clinically defined repression, including the increasing pressure which makes it likely that "needs may erupt into turbulent upheavals and expressions of pent-up feelings."[5]

Feeling and Conscious (Repressed) Literalism: World B

Again ontogenetically speaking, it should be noted that it is in youth that we allow ourselves to feel most intensely. Tillich maintains that in the moment when the questioning mind breaks the natural acceptance of the mythological visions of ultimacy as literal (most often occurring in adolescence), one is forced into one of two new ways of relating to symbols. The first way is actually a second stage of literalism, which he calls conscious or repressed literalism.[6] The second way, seen in this study as being in a developmental sequence and as following conscious literalism, is presented in chapter 14.

When a literal understanding of symbol and myth is

confronted by what can be verified through observation and experiment in such a way as to cast doubt upon that concreteness, one is thrust into World B. If the newly arrived World B person cannot or will not take on the anxiety of uncertainty that is a part of relating to symbols as symbols—that is, in a nonliteral manner—the awareness of the questions and their inherent problems remains, but it is half consciously, half unconsciously, repressed. "The tool of repression is usually an acknowledged authority with sacred qualities like the Church or the Bible, to which one owes unconditional surrender."[7]

The person who had no problem accepting Creation as an act that took place in the course of a week may now experience a profound sense of anxiety when faced with the geological evidence that conflicts with a literal interpretation of the Creation accounts. At the conscious stage of literalism, in World B, the anxiety is handled by receiving an answer from the sacred authority that allows the Creation accounts to be accepted literally again. Any remaining anxiety is repressed. This stage, like the first, is, according to Tillich, still justifiable if the questioning power is very weak and can be answered easily.

Feeling/World B Illuminative Case

A chaplain's late afternoon reverie evaporated with the jangling phone. Obstetrics and Gynecology was calling.

"There's a lady up here who's been in labor for eighteen hours. She's asking for a chaplain. Can you come?"

"Sure."

He was met at the labor-room door by a doctor and a nurse who indicated that they had tried everything in the book, to no avail. Barely concealing their amusement, they added, "Now she wants to try prayer," and ushered him in.

"Here's the chaplain. He's going to pray for you."

After a brief get-acquainted talk, the chaplain offered his prayer.

Father, we ask that your loving presence be felt in a very real way by this, your child, as she struggles in the pangs of her own child's birth. We're grateful that you are with us, wherever life's circumstances may take us; that no matter what happens to us, we have your promise that you'll never leave us comfortless, either now or forevermore. We pray this prayer in the name of your Son, the Great Physician himself, our Saviour and Lord Jesus Christ. Amen.

Twenty minutes later she gave birth to a fine, healthy boy. The lady stalled in labor was clearly in World B. In her conscious literalism she wished to turn her problem over to an acknowledged authority with sacred qualities—the chaplain. She managed to do so, and once that had been accomplished, and the sacred authority had addressed God in her presence, in her behalf, her anxiety was diminished sufficiently for her to relax and have her baby.

CHAPTER 14

THINKING AND CONSCIOUSNESS OF THE ULTIMATE

The Thinking Typology

Whereas the sensation type focuses upon the present, and the feeling type upon the past, the thinking type structures time in a linear progression: A particular past act led to this present act; this present act should therefore lead to a particular future act. This orderly, sequential sense of time is the basis for several thinking-type characteristics: great respect for proper timing; constant evaluation of progress; a love of history, with a corresponding sense of place in it; and a dread of wasted time.

Not surprisingly, the thinking type enjoys—even craves—originating ideas, thinking logically, theorizing, and synthesizing the components of a problem. A general disposition toward "why" questions requires at least the occasional random input of new information, to avoid the tendency to slip into a rut in which the same questions and thoughts are repeated again and again. Another need is time alone to think.

Truth is a central commitment for thinking-differentiated persons. Malone says that "truth" is the one word summarizing the thing of greatest value to a thinking type.[1]

A second commitment, related to the first, is to principles. In deciding how to respond to a new situation, the thinking type looks for the principles involved. With experience, these principles become so strongly embedded as to be inviolable. History records the martyrdom of thinking types who chose death rather than renounce a high principle or what they perceived to be the truth. Thus there is great stress when this type experiences a conflict between principles.

A third basic commitment is to justice. As with the first two, this commitment is carried out on an impersonal basis. The thinking type has minimal difficulty divorcing personal feelings or relationships from necessary actions in the cause of justice.

Thinking types prefer to let ideas generate feelings, not vice versa, and to protect themselves from a particular vulnerability to a reversal of that order—feelings "out of control"—by intellectualizing, losing access to emotions, avoidance, and by resolving emotion-charged problems as quickly as possible.

In general, thinking types are dispassionate, self-critical, deliberate, persistent, careful managers, willing to delegate authority, able to work within the system, approval-seeking, ambitious, very competitive, witty, headstrong, scholarly (though not necessarily extremely intelligent), and highly verbal, with tendencies toward righteous indignation, fanaticism, merciless retaliation, and pomposity.

In the thinking category, Malone places Plato, Aristotle, Augustus Caesar, Thomas Aquinas, Erasmus, Martin Luther, John Milton, Frederick Nietzsche, Abraham Lincoln, Karl Marx, Woodrow Wilson, Albert Einstein, Sigmund Freud, Franklin D. Roosevelt, Jean-Paul Sartre, Charles DeGaulle, Lillian Hellman, W. H. Auden, and John F. Kennedy.[2]

The Thinking Type and Systematic Theology

The thinking type, then, becomes conscious of reality within an orderly, past-present-future, linear concept of time; thrives on ideas; and is committed to high principles, such as truth and justice. Consequently, those thinking types who attempt to become conscious of the ultimate via sacred forms find their greatest satisfaction in the concerns of systematic theology, a branch of theology which,

THINKING

according to Webster, "attempts to reduce all religious truth to statements forming a self-consistent and organized whole."

Theology derives from two Greek words: *Theos*, meaning God, and *logos*, meaning word or rational thought. Its ongoing task is to translate the truths of religion/faith into understandable terms for each generation. In his rationale for his layman's guide to Protestant Christian theology, William E. Hordern maintains that the choice is between a well-thought-out theology, which passes the tests of critical thought, and a "hodgepodge theology of unexamined concepts, prejudices, and feelings" (not a choice between theology and no theology).[3]

In this sense each person is a theologian. The discipline is not limited to people such as Thomas Aquinas, John Calvin, and Karl Barth.

Frequently someone says: "Why bother with theology? The theologians waste their time debating unimportant issues." Let us examine this statement. Why are these issues deemed unimportant? Obviously, the objector has in mind some concept of highest value by which he judges the arguments of theologians valueless. He has a theological position, a belief about the nature of God, which leads him to judge as unimportant the arguments of theologians. In short, even this attack upon theology is a theological attack.[4]

Thinking and Broken Myth: World C

From an ontogenic point of view, Tillich's second new way of relating to symbol and myth (once the questioning mind breaks the natural acceptance of mythological visions)—broken myth—requires the ability to think abstractly, a capability fully developed only in late adolescence or early adulthood. Broken myth (or symbol) is a myth (or a symbol) "which is understood as a myth [or a symbol] but is not removed or replaced."[5] To see a myth as a myth or a symbol as a symbol is to recognize it as something pointing beyond itself while participating in that to which it points.

The reason a myth or a symbol is not removed or replaced is because nothing else can take its place. Nothing else "points beyond itself . . . participates in that to which it points . . . opens up levels of reality which otherwise are closed . . . unlocks dimensions and elements of our soul which correspond to the dimensions and elements of reality [opened by myth or symbol] . . . and grow[s] out of the individual or collective unconscious."[6] Nothing but a myth or a symbol is able to express the ultimate.

An individual operating in World C retains the language of myth—the anthropomorphic image, the historical setting—because without them that individual has no language at all with which to speak about ultimate concern. A World C person breaks the code and gets the message. Although the code is not the message, the World C resident recognizes that without the code the message cannot be received. One still speaks of the second day of Creation, for example, because the myth conveys something about the ultimate that only myth can, but there is no problem when mythical truth encounters geological fact. Myth addresses the nature of the ultimate, while geology attends to that which is less than ultimate—the age of the earth.

That is not to say that one who replaces the unbroken myth of literalism with the broken myth is without problems. It is the World A person, operating within the security of natural literalism, who has no problems (or at least recognizes no problems) and thus has no anxiety. The World B individual has this problem: In the second stage of literalism, the system of repression constantly must be reinforced and fed by unconditional surrender to the authority. Conflicting authority cannot be recognized, much less tolerated. If the repression works well enough, the literalist again feels certain.

The World C problem—that caused by the break in literal understanding of myth—is a constant uncertainty that cannot be relieved by the magic of natural literalism or by the sacred authority of conscious literalism. World C uncertainty can be answered only with faith and courage. Although faith and courage conquer uncertainty (doubt), they cannot eliminate it. "Courage does not deny that there is doubt, but it takes the doubt into itself as an expression of its own finitude and affirms the content of an ultimate concern. Courage does not need the safety of an unquestionable conviction. It includes the risk without which no creative life is possible."[7]

Thinking/World C Illuminative Case

The chaplain of Baptist beliefs and upbringing made last minute adjustments in his notes for the Sunday morning chapel service. Then the call came from Newborn Nursery.

"We have twins only hours old, and one of them isn't expected to live. The parents are asking that they be baptized."

Anxious for more than one reason, the chaplain stalled. "Any particular denomination?" But he knew he could not bounce-pass this one, anyway, since all the other ministers were in the midst of conducting their own services.

"No. They don't have any particular denominational preference. They just want their babies baptized before one of them dies."

"Do you think the critical one can last 'til I get through our service? That'll be about half an hour."

"Yes, I think so."

The chaplain had made up his mind during this exchange to proceed, after ten years of ministry, to do his first infant baptism, and to do it by a mode other than immersion. To his amazement, the chaplain later discovered that the parents had asked for the baptism not out of their own belief, a sort of respectful skepticism, but to ease the minds of the grandparents, who were dedicated church people.

The baptism request, coming as it did on Sunday morning, actually served to precipitate the Baptist chaplain's arrival in World C. Forced by circumstances into making a decision either on the basis of an external acknowledged authority with sacred qualities (Baptist doctrine), or on an internal, broken-symbol basis (the symbol of believers' baptism by immersion), he chose the latter. After the baptisms, he found himself sharing his awkwardness with people who turned out to be World C parents, trying to exercise pastoral care themselves, via what was for them a broken symbol (baptism), to ease the suffering of the infants' World B grandparents, for whom baptism was a very literal symbol.

CHAPTER 15

INTUITION AND CONSCIOUSNESS OF THE ULTIMATE

The Intuition Typology

With regard to time, sensation types center upon the present; feeling types, upon the past; thinking types, upon a logical linear progression from past to present to future; and intuition types, upon the future, almost to the exclusion of past and present. Intuitives invest three qualities into this focus upon the future.

First, the vision: Not necessarily mystical (though William Blake's vision was), nor fantastic (though Marc Chagall's was), nor unearthly (though Mary Baker Eddy's was), the intuitive vision is "the desire of the imagination and the will that becomes synonymous with the personhood of the believer and is therefore perceived as reality."[1] Such a vision may concern anything, from God (Mary Baker Eddy), to the dance (Isadora Duncan), to a perfect love (Queen Victoria). It is far-reaching, bigger than life, and should not be confused with more immediate minivisions about careers, relationships, or current events.

Second, the imagination: Under stress, sensation types act, feeling types explore their emotions, thinking types plan, and intuition types turn to their imaginations. Not to be confused with creativity, a quality that cuts across typological lines, imagination can produce many zany schemes for each truly innovative plan. When others' imaginations are sufficiently stirred, the intuitive is hailed as a prophet. If not, the intuitive may be written off as a crazy inventor, or on occasion, institutionalized (as in the case of Ezra Pound).

Third, the charisma—the ability to arouse the imagination and commitment of others regarding the imaginative vision. Inspired by the vision, the charismatic intuitive inspires followers. Adolph Hitler, Napoleon Bonaparte, and Patrick Henry are some notable historical examples of individuals with the ability to implement their vision in such a way that people can be moved to respond with their energies and even with their very lives.

In general, intuitives are optimistic, keeping open as many options as possible and seeing whatever is possible as real; they are continually theorizing and generalizing, linking everything into an overall connection of central truths of universal significance; their enthusiasm is often disproportionate to their skill; they agonize over the failure of a crucial vision; there is a tendency to believe deeply in cosmic forces that affect their destinies; they have a propensity to play God. They are often shy, playful, eccentric, vicious, and moody.

Malone lists Alexander the Great, Nero, Sir Walter Raleigh, Mary Queen of Scots, Patrick Henry, Marie Antoinette, William Blake, Ludwig von Beethoven, Emily Bronte, Queen Victoria, Richard Wagner, Carl Jung, Napoleon Bonaparte, Ezra Pound, Mary Baker Eddy, Rudolph Valentino, Leon Trotsky, Adolph Hitler, Marc Chagall, Isadora Duncan, and James Joyce as intuition types.[2]

The Intuition Type and the Religious Quest

The intuition type consciously appropriates reality within a futuristic framework involving a central vision, imaginatively created and charismatically sustained in highly individualistic and often antireligious fashion. Therefore, those intuitives who attempt to consciously appropriate ultimacy through religious forms are extremely difficult to identify. Here the psychology of religion offers aid, with the application of inductive methods to the study of religious phenomena. William James' concept of "once born" and "twice born," in *Varieties of Religious Experience*, first presented as the Gifford Lectures in 1901–1902 and making use of the idiographic method, was the classic early example of the effort to find meaningful categories for religious belief, experience, and behavior.

A more recent, near-classic attempt to categorize religious experience is that of Gordon W. Allport. In *The Individual and His Religion* (1950), one can find the beginnings of his thought that later developed the categories of intrinsic and extrinsic religion. His list of attributes that delineate the mature religious sentiment: well differentiated, dynamic, productive of a consistent morality, comprehensive, integral, and basically heuristic, later seem to describe the intrinsically motivated person.[3]

In a series of studies reported in journal articles from 1959 until 1967, Allport refined his categories. For Allport, the intrinsically religious person *lives* his religion; religion is *an end in itself*, the point around which other concerns are arranged. Having adopted a creed, the intrinsically motivated individual seeks to internalize it and follow it to the fullest extent. The extrinsically religious person, on the other hand, *uses* his religion; religion is *a means to ends*, such as sociability, security, or status.

Even more recent studies challenge the adequacy of the intrinsic/extrinsic dichotomy. They point out that the intrinsic believer, at first described as "a reflexive, critical, highly differentiated, sincere, humble person, who thought for himself, who cared, and who put his beliefs into action," later manifests "dispositions which might characterize a compulsive, conforming, and unquestioning 'true believer.'"[4]

Even as Allport pointed out two distinct religious orientations that had been confounded in earlier research, C. Daniel Batson contends that two different orientations have been confounded and confused within Allport's concept of the intrinsically religious person.

In addition to the true believer of the intrinsic dimension of the Religious Orientation Scale, there are individuals who orient to religion as a quest. These persons view religion as an endless process of probing and questioning generated by the tensions, contradictions, and tragedies in their own lives and in society. Not necessarily aligned with any formal religious institution or creed, they are continually raising ultimate "whys," both about the existing social structure and about the structure of life itself. While it may seem strange to call such an individual religious, there is actually a long history of such a view. It goes at least as far back in Western thought as the Hebrew prophets and much farther back in Eastern religions.[5]

In a complex research design, Batson created two new psychometric instruments—the "religious life inventory" and the "doctrinal orthodoxy scale"—which he administered to several groups of subjects, together with the two subscales of Allport's "religious orientation scale." He hypothesized that these measures would combine to form a three-dimensional measure of religious orientation—religion as a means (extrinsic), religion as an end (intrinsic), and religion as a quest. He concluded that "the present research provided preliminary validating evidence for the conceptual utility of a three dimensional model."[6]

Intuition and the Monomyth: World D

Certain World C individuals grow weary of breaking the code to get the message, and they find that speaking at all of the second day of Creation, for example, is increasingly meaningless. At this point such persons step beyond the solid three-category Tillichian framework, out into the unknown. They have become new citizens of World D; they have become questers, and in that quest they embody what James Joyce called the monomyth.

Ontogenetically, the quest orientation has a paradoxical affinity for both age and infancy: age, in that the quest itself is a profoundly maturing journey; infancy, in that, as Jung points out, in common with sensation, intuition is "a characteristic of infantile and primitive psychology."[7] Perhaps this bonding of old and new makes possible a cyclical closure in an otherwise exclusively linear ontogenic progression, as seen in the special rapport that the very old seem to have with the very young.

CONSCIOUSNESS AND THE ULTIMATE

What is the nature of the quest? What myth, mono- or any other, can it be said that questors live out in their journeys?

> A hero ventures forth from the world of common day into a region of supernatural wonder: fabulous forces are there encountered and a decisive victory is won: the hero comes back from this mysterious adventure with the power to bestow boons on his fellow man.[8]

Joseph Campbell has written convincingly that the myths of the world, despite the infinite variety of setting, incident, and costume, offer only a limited number of responses to the riddle of life. He goes on to describe a composite hero-myth, defined in its essence in the quoted passage, and discusses its elements: the call to adventure, refusal of the call, supernatural aid, the crossing of the first threshold, the belly of the whale, the road of trials, the meeting with the goddess, woman as temptress, atonement with the father, apotheosis, the ultimate boon, refusal of the return, the magic flight, rescue from without, and the crossing of the return threshold, the hero now becoming master of the two worlds.

These two worlds, the human and the divine, can be depicted only as different from each other. However, if the hero-circuit is completed—if the hero returns from the adventure—he is living proof (a great key to the understanding of myth and symbol) that the two worlds are actually one.

> The realm of the gods is a forgotten dimension of the world we know. And the exploration of that dimension, either willingly or unwillingly, is the whole sense of the deed of the hero. The values and distinctions that in normal life seem important disappear with the terrifying assimilation of the self into what formerly was only otherness.[9]

Intuition/World D Illuminative Case

A thirty-seven-year-old, five-years-divorced, Protestant public-school speech clinician applied for admission to a supervised ministry program for parish clergy. She never

INTUITION

had considered becoming a minister, but an acquaintance had told her the course would allow introspection, interaction with clients, and improvement of communication and caring skills. During the interview process the following data came to light.

The oldest of three children born to a hard-working Midwest farm couple, she had been bored by the small church she was expected to attend (already World C?). She decided to break with her small community and circle of friends to go to a larger high school in a nearby town, at a time when most adolescents would rather die than move—just before her senior year (the call to adventure?). Later, after two basically pleasant and successful years of college, she again chose new horizons—work in a large city (the World D crossing of the first threshold?). After a while she once more "grew restless," became a stewardess and, of course, traveled extensively (the road of trials?).

She met (the meeting with the god?) and married a young executive (man as the tempter?). During the next six years she studied speech pathology, completed her degree work and clinical training, questioned "whether my marriage was nurturing me emotionally and spiritually," decided after counseling that it was not, and was divorced. When she moved into her own apartment, she experienced a sense of freedom and adventure. "I wanted to develop my soul, my spirit longed for food, for nourishment."

She became interested in Jungian therapy, nutrition, and wholistic health. She resigned her job and began to lose weight and sleep. Her parents insisted upon taking her home to recuperate, and she reluctantly agreed (atonement with the mother?). After regaining her health, she resumed the quest, writing of experiences with shiatsu, Touch for Health, acupuncture, aptos, Kara, and spiritual retreat, a search that continues to this writing.

PART III

THEOLOGY:
A CHRISTOLOGICAL PRESCRIPTION FOR CONSCIOUSNESS OF THE ULTIMATE

CHAPTER 16

A CHRISTOLOGICAL SURVEY

From Phylogeny to Ontogeny to Christology

Phylogeny, the historical account of the developing consciousness of the ultimate, has led to a crossroads. Humanity faces a stark choice. One route leads to actualization of the beatific vision—convergence upon the Omega Point, the bringing to fulfillment of human potential in a creative unity of the universal and the personal. The other route points in the opposite direction—to the self-induced destruction of humanity.

Ontogeny, the psychological study of individual consciousness of the ultimate, suggests only one of four currently discernible stages, intuition, as primarily future-oriented. Furthermore, this type is seen sequentially as the last of the four (World D), with the strong implication that it is therefore probably the smallest of the four categories in terms of numbers of persons so classified.[1]

When posited side by side, the phylogenetic and ontogenetic findings point to an alarming conclusion: Among the persons who consciously seek the ultimate at the current historical crossroads, those most psychologically attuned to future concerns are the most scarce and, as previously noted, the hardest to identify.

In order to avoid reliance primarily upon chance (unconscious) attempts to deal with such ultimate concerns at this critical juncture, faith resources must be brought to bear with the greatest urgency. Can Christian theology speak meaningfully and forcefully to the crossroads situation? Since for Christianity the doctrine of Jesus Christ is central, a sampling of representative Christologies is a necessary preliminary to the formulation of an answer.[2]

Jesus Christ: Very God and Very Man (Orthodoxy)

"The central statement of the Christology of the early Church is that God becomes one with man: Jesus Christ 'very God and very man'."[3] As framed and adopted by the Council of Chalcedon in A.D. 451, the *Definitio fidei* was destined to become the common ground upon which the majority of later Christians could stand, even when disagreeing ecclesiastically. It reads, in part:

In agreement, therefore, with the holy fathers, we all unanimously teach that we should confess that our Lord Jesus Christ is one and the same Son, the same perfect in Godhead and the same perfect in manhood, truly God and truly man, the same of a rational soul and body, consubstantial with the Father in Godhead, and the same consubstantial with us in manhood.[4]

This once-and-for-all pivotal historical event—this mystery of one person, one body encompassing two fully complete natures "unconfusedly, unchangeably, indivisibly, and inseparably," as affirmed by more than five hundred bishops that October day—amplified the Nicean Creed (325) to cope with Nestorian and Eutychian heresies so effectively that *Definitio fiedi* stands to this day as the orthodox Christian solution to the christological problem.

The Christology of Divine Self-Limitation (Kenotic Theory)

Chalcedonian Christology gained such a high degree of authority in both the Eastern Orthodox and Roman Catholic traditions (despite early Monophysite separations and the theological stance of Constantinople II) that most Protestant

Reformers even upheld it. Not until the nineteenth century did a major alternative emerge within Protestantism.

According to Gottfried Thomasius of Erlangen (1802–1875), the Incarnation of Jesus Christ was not only his "assumption of human nature" but also "the self-limitation of the Son of God." There are, therefore, two states of the God/Man—humiliation and exaltation—and they are connected by death. In the first state, "immanent divine attributes" of truth, holiness, self-determination, and love are revealed, but the Son of God is divested of the "relative divine attributes" of omnipresence, omniscience, and omnipotence, in his kenosis, or self-emptying (see Phil. 2:7). In the second state those relative attributes are repossessed.[5]

Peter Taylor Forsyth (1848–1921) and Hugh Ross Mackintosh (1870–1936) further refined the theory: Forsyth distinguished kenosis (self-emptying) from plerosis (self-fulfillment); Mackintosh, the actuality of immanent divine attributes from their potency. Where the *Definito fidei* understands Jesus Christ in terms of two natures, divine and human, in one person, the Christology of divine self-limitation understands him in two movements, humiliation and glorification.[6]

The Initiator of the Kingdom of God (Liberalism; The Social Gospel)

Walter Rauschenbusch (1861–1918), proponent of the social gospel, represents the liberal reaction against what it perceived as the orthodox denial of the real spiritual, moral, and rational humanity of Jesus; against the "God in a human body" and overemphasis upon the supernatural nature and substitutionary work of the one and only Savior of the world. Such a Christ seemed irrelevant to Rauschenbusch and his poor parishioners in a New York City ghetto. Out of his sense of social injustice grew his Christology of Jesus' full humanity, in which he saw Jesus' personality and life, not as an effortless divine inheritance, but rather as achieved within the tangle of hard moral questions, sore temptations, and intense struggles that Jesus experienced.

Thus for liberals like Rauschenbusch, Jesus Christ illustrates the human life of faith, symbolizes the divine resources available, and inspires personal commitment more by his life than by his death; more when his words/deeds are separated from primitive Christianity's language and theology.[7]

The social gospel would interpret all the events of his life, including his death, by the dominant purpose which he consistently followed, the establishment of the Kingdom of God. This is the only interpretation which would have appealed to himself. His life was what counted; his death was part of it. The historic current of salvation which went out from him is the prolongation of that life into which he put his conscious energy.[8]

Jesus Christ: The Lord as Servant and the Servant as Lord (Neo-orthodoxy)

Karl Barth (1886–1968), described by his peers as the most creative Protestant theologian since John Calvin, relates every part of his massive fourteen-volume *Church Dogmatics* to a christological center. His theology, which others labeled as neo-orthodoxy (a term he deplored), affirms (with liberalism) Jesus Christ as a thoroughly human, independent self and upholds (with orthodoxy) humanity's inabilty to find God apart from Jesus Christ. Barth makes a sharp distinction between the Christ of faith and the Jesus of history, redefining the two natures of Jesus Christ in terms of two distinct levels of that one historic event.[9] He sees this as building upon, not avoiding, the Chalcedonian formula. "Jesus Christ is not what He is—very God, very man, very God-man—in order as such to mean and do and accomplish something else which is atonement. But His being as God and man and God-man consists in the completed act of the reconciliation of man with God."[10] Thus Barth tries to guard against the *Definito fidei* interpretation of Jesus Christ as a static essence; rather, he is an action of God—the determinative center of cosmic and human destiny. His person and work cannot be meaningfully separated, even for the purpose of study.[11]

A CHRISTOLOGICAL SURVEY

In face of the history which took place in Jesus Christ the New Testament says that these two elements of the one grace, the divine and the human, are one in Him, not one form but in two. . . . When, therefore, the later Christology safeguarded against any confusion or transmutation of the two natures the one into the other and therefore into a third, the innovation was not one of substance but only of theology, and one which the substance itself demanded.[12]

Jesus Christ and the New Being (Theology of Culture)

Paul Tillich (1886-1965), in his *Systematic Theology*, introduces his doctrine of God by defining him as Being itself—as the power and ground of being—and calls Jesus Christ the manifestation of the New Being. Humanity suffers from existential estrangement and bondage of the will. Relief is sought in the quest for new being. Western religion in general has looked for new being within the historical process. Christianity in particular has found it within that process, in a personal life; or rather, it has been given through Jesus as the Christ, the bearer of the new being as expressed in his words (the Word), his deeds (inseparable from his being), and his suffering (including his violent death as "a consequence of the inescapable conflict between the forces of existential estrangement and the bearer of that by which existence is conquered").[13]

New Being is essential being under the conditions of existence, conquering the gap between essence and existence. . . . The New Being is new insofar as it is the undistorted manifestation of essential being within and under the conditions of existence. It is new in two respects: it is new in contrast to the merely potential character of essential being; and it is new over against the estranged character of existential being. It is actual, conquering the estrangement of actual existence.[14]

Thus for Tillich, Jesus Christ keeps a "permanent unity" with God, while subjected to all that existential estrangement entails. The negativities of existence are accepted; they are transcended by the power of that unity.

CONSCIOUSNESS AND THE ULTIMATE

The Incarnation in Process Theology (Process Thought)

Whereas all the Christologies summarized have philosphically assumed (from classical metaphysics) that being, or substance, is the widest, most inclusive category for understanding anything real, the Incarnation in process theology does not so assume. To the contrary, process theology appeals to process philosophy, in which the greatest category for understanding reality is "becoming," not "being"; process, not substance. Here God is not seen as a being outside time, but rather as an eternal actual entity, the "Principle of Concretion," the "Category of the Ultimate," immanent in every pulse of experience through his "consequent" nature, which is derived from his all-embracing "primordial" (hidden) nature.[15]

Various process theologians have their favorite christological images. For Bernard E. Meland, it is the New Creation.[16] For Teilhard de Chardin, it is the Cosmic Christ, identical with his Omega (the Universal Element).[17] For W. Norman Pittenger, it is a union analogous to marriage.

> The most complete, the fullest, the most organic and integrated union of Godhead and manhood which is conceivable is precisely one in which by gracious indwelling of God in man and by manhood's free response in surrender and love, there is established a relationship which is neither accidental nor incidental, on the one hand, nor mechanical and physical, on the other; but a full, free, gracious unity of the two in Jesus Christ, who is both the farthest reach of God The Word into the life of man and also (and by consequence) the richest response of man to God.[18]

Eschatological Christology (Eschatological Theology)

Wolfhart Pannenberg (b. 1928) builds his Christology "from below"—that is, from the historical reality of the man Jesus. To begin from above would not take into consideration the fact that his divinity is neither self-evident or self-explanatory to modern man. Thus Pannenberg looks at Jesus' office and finds that it is "to call men into the

Kingdom of God, which had appeared with him." This presupposes God's election of Israel and the apocalyptic expectation of the future revelation of God's glory. Through his office and his call, Jesus claimed divine authority. However, "Jesus' unity with God was not yet established by the claim implied in his pre-Easter appearance, but only by his resurrection from the dead."[19]

For Pannenberg, then, the destiny of Jesus Christ—his crucifixion and resurrection—are central. He rejects the historicity of Jesus' "embracing" of death, in favor of the view that the fatal trip to Jerusalem was more an attempt "to bring about a decision regarding his claim concerning the nearness of God's Kingdom and the centrality of his person in the anticipation of it."[20]

His execution as a rebel and messianic pretender was not, for Pannenberg, the end of Jesus' history. After careful consideration, he concludes:

Thus the resurrection of Jesus would be designated as a historical event in this sense: If the emergence of primitive Christianity, which, apart from other traditions, is also traced back by Paul to appearances of the resurrected Jesus, can be understood in spite of all critical examination of the tradition only if one examines it in the light of the eschatological hope for a resurrection from the dead, then that which is so designated (Jesus' resurrection) is a historical event, even if we do not know anything more particlar about it. Then an event that is expressible only in the language of the eschatological expectation is to be asserted as a historical occurrence.[21]

Moving then from a Christology "from below" to a Christology "from before," Pannenberg holds that just as the historical event of Jesus' resurrection confirmed his proclamation of the coming kingdom of God and explained his unity with God (not in the old sense of adoption, receiving divinity only in the resurrection, since that obscures the *confirmatory* nature of the Easter event), so it is a preview (prolepsis) of the end of all history. ". . . The eschatological function of Jesus as the anticipation of God's future forms the key to the central theme of Incarnation."[22]

CONSCIOUSNESS AND THE ULTIMATE

Jesus Christ as the Self-Annihilation of God (Death-of-God Theology)

Thomas J. J. Altizer (b. 1927), the boldest of the death-of-God theologians, takes kenotic theory to its extreme, holding that God emptied himself completely into Jesus Christ and that he "actually died in Christ," in a historical and cosmic movement of the sacred into the profane, from transcendence to immanence, from innocence to experience. The radical Christian affirms that God has died in Christ; that the death of God is a final, irrevocable event and is the historical realization of the dawning of the kingdom of God. How does the Christian know this?

Because the Christian lives in the fully incarnate body of Christ, he acknowledges the totality of our experience as the consummation of the kenotic passion of the Word, and by giving himself to the Christ who is present to us he is liberated from the alien power of an emptied and darkened transcendence. Rather than being mute and numb in response to the advent of a world in which the original name of God is no longer sayable, the Christian can live and speak by pronouncing the word of God's death, by joyously announcing the "good news" of the death of God, and by greeting the naked reality of our experience as the triumphant realization of the self-negation of God.[23]

Jesus Christ as Harlequin (Theology of Juxtaposition)

In *The Feast of Fools*, Harvey Cox proposes a theological juxtaposition in which a creative tension is sought. Why not celebrate "the collision of symbol and situation as the occasion for new experience and unprecedented perception," he asks. A theology of juxtaposition could "play off the tensions" of traditional theology's faith emphasis upon the past, radical theology's focus on the present faith crisis, and eschatological theology's faith in a future hope. At the center of Cox's proposal for a theology of juxtaposition is a startling Christology.

Now in the new, or really an old but recaptured guise, Christ has made an unexpected entrance onto the stage of modern secular

A CHRISTOLOGICAL SURVEY

life. Enter Christ the harlequin: the personification of festivity and fantasy in an age that had almost lost both. Coming now in grease paint and halo, this Christ is able to touch our jaded modern consciousness as other images of Christ cannot.[24]

From his day's fascination with such imagination-capturing clowns as Charlie Chaplin, Buster Keaton, and the Marx Brothers, Cox backtracks the historical thread of absurdity in Christianity to the catacomb Christians' depiction of a crucified human figure with the head of an ass, and even points up the biblical bases: Jesus rode into Jerusalem on a donkey and later was costumed by his executioners in royal garb and a crown of thorns. Cox sees as only fitting that in the present secularized "post-Christian era," an often weak-appearing, "even ridiculous church, somehow peculiarly at odds with the ruling assumptions of its day, once again can appreciate the harlequinesque Christ. His pathos, his weakness, his irony—all begin to make a strange kind of sense again."[25]

CHAPTER 17

A CHRISTOLOGICAL CRITIQUE

A Critique of Orthodoxy

Any word spoken in response to the crossroads situation from within the specific context of the orthodox solution to the christological problem (Jesus Christ, very God, very Man) is severely weakened by an awareness of its long, uneven etiology. The formula affirmed by the bishops gathered at Chalcedon marked only a point of consensus in an ongoing process of understandings about Jesus Christ, a process of interpretation which is the continuing task of Christian theology in each generation.

The very earliest Christology was messianic. Jesus' followers saw him as the Messiah of the Jewish hope, minus the earthly exaltation contained within that hope (explained by identification of Jesus with the suffering servant of Isa. 53:5). Paul followed shortly afterward, and though he taught Christ's unity in character with God, he never flatly called Christ "God."

A half generation after the death of Paul a differing interpretation appeared in the earliest written Gospel, that of Mark. No thought is given there to the preexistence of Jesus, and he is presented as the Son of God by adoption at the time of his baptism (Mark 1:9-11). Along with Jesus' humiliation appears a new note of glory within his earthly life (see 1:24, 3:12, 9:2-8).

The next two Gospels, Matthew and Luke, seeming almost like correctives to Mark, date the manifestation of

Christ's divine Sonship from his conception (supernatural) and birth (natural, but with supernatural accoutrements), and continue to develop the exaltation-while-still-on-earth theme. The Gospel of John, appearing at the turn of the first century, became at last formative of what was to become orthodoxy, by identifying Christ with the preexistent Stoic Logos; by carrying the first three Gospels' glorification much further (no more an anguished cry from the cross; not even the pathetic prayer in Gethsemane remains); and even by allowing the triumphant Christ to remember his preexistence (17:5).

All that can be meaningfully salvaged from the ancient formula *Definitio fidei* for use in response to the crossroads situation is the assumption upon which the formula itself was based—that the Christ-event was a once-and-for-all pivotal event in the history of humanity and therefore is uniquely involved in humanity's efforts to become more conscious of the ultimate.

A Critique of Kenotic Theory

Kenotic theory's contribution, in response to the crossroads situation, suffers from credibility problems similar to those of the orthodox christological solution, in that it, too, is based on intellectual refinements made in the ongoing process of understandings about Jesus Christ. It, too, assumes the preexistence of Christ. In addition, it conceptualizes a Godhead capable of temporarily setting aside some capabilities while emptying itself into the form of a human being (humiliation), only to reclaim them in the second phase (exaltation)—too heady, too mathematical, too equationlike.

The feature most transferable to a christological stance pertinent to the crossroads situation is that of emptying. Something was poured out, emptied. Something precious. Precisely what that something was may become more clear in the next chapter, in the christological prescription for the crossroads situation, from the level of consciousness of the ultimate achieved thus far by human beings.

CONSCIOUSNESS AND THE ULTIMATE

A Critique of Liberalism

Liberalism's lifting up of the life of Jesus Christ as a model for all humanity to follow (even though it may have been a necessary corrective to the orthodox tendency to downplay Jesus' humanity) lacks force as a response to the crossroads situation. Why? Because advocates of other great names in history could make convincing cases that their candidates, too, should be seen as equally inspiring models from which an adequate response to the crossroads situation could spring. For example, why not Gautama Buddha? Or Muhammad? Michael Hart, in his book *The 100: A Ranking of the Most Influential Persons in History*, ranks Muhammad as the single most influential person who ever lived (Jesus Christ is third; Gautama Buddha, fourth) because of his unparalleled combination of both secular (unifier of Arab tribesmen into a force that carved out an empire stretching from the Atlantic Ocean to India) and religious (author of the Koran) influence.

One feature of liberalism that must be incorporated into a truly meaningful christological response to the crossroads situation, however, is the social-action aspect. The Christian, inspired by Christ's example, engages in *acts* designed to carry out Christ's teachings: Love one's neighbor through kindly good works; attempt to overcome social injustices and inequities, and so forth.

A Critique of Neo-orthodoxy

Any word spoken by Barthian neo-orthodoxy to the crossroads situation is likely to be heard and appreciated only by those persons who are identified already as Christians and who, furthermore, affirm the objective authority of the Bible as God's Word to and about man. For Barth, Christology and all other dogmatics (official teachings of the church) are conversations that take place within the church. Barth's work is not apologetic; it courageously assumes that Christianity can stand on its own two feet, using only its own norm—the Bible. Unfortunately, today's Christian is also a product of the modern world; the problem of unbelief is therefore found within, as well as outside the church. Thus Barth's steadfast (if admirable) refusal to allow input into his Christology from history, psychology, sociology, and other knowledge, greatly weakens his contribution to Christology for the crossroads situation.

That which *is* viable and therefore becomes the neo-orthodox strength to be incorporated into a christological prescription for the crossroads situation is this: A saving Word somehow has been expressed in Jesus Christ and therefore the message is there, to be translated afresh.

A Critique of the Theology of Culture

Tillich's definition of God as Being itself—as the power and the ground of being—places his theological system alongside the others critiqued thus far and thereby leaves it open to the criticisms leveled upon classical metaphysics by nominalist and process philosophy. Metaphysics assumes being, or substance, to be the most inclusive category for understanding anything real.

Tillich adroitly sidesteps the nominalist criticism by claiming that for him, the concept of being is less an abstract, universal category than an "explanation of the experience of being over against non-being."[1]

Not so for process criticism, which assumes becoming, or process, to be the most inclusive category. Any system so firmly based in being—any Christology of being in general, and Tillich's new being in particular—becomes buried in the rubble of what has been described as the collapse of the three-storied universe.[2] Despite the attempts of Tillich and his defenders to bring new meanings to such terms as "the ground of being," they remain finally just as spatially bound and, unfortunately, just as difficult for any honest citizen of the modern world to visualize, as are such images as God-up-there or God-out-there.

What *can* be carried forward from Tillich's Christ in the new being is not the "being," but the "new." Something new did occur in Jesus Christ. However, only recently has the religious consciousness of humanity been sufficiently developed that a focus for that something new can emerge in the crossroads situation. This focus will be more fully developed in chapter 18.

A Critique of Process Thought

The most obvious difficulty with process thought as applied to Christian theology is its lack of coherence. Each interpreter brings his own interpretation and concepts to A. N. Whitehead's complex philosophy: Hartshorne's dipolar God (abstract and absolute versus concrete and relative) and panentheism (God includes the world while transcending it); Williams' perspectives; Loomer's co-dependents; and Wieman's God, a kind of process taking place between humans.

There are vital questions unanswered. Is God a single actual entity or a personally ordered society of actual entities? How can God be involved in experiences from every standpoint, yet be unified eternally? How account for the presence of evil, while God is seeking to lure the world toward more desirable forms of order? And, with specific regard to Christology, is it enough that the only difference between Jesus Christ and all other instances of divine operation in humanity is one of degree, not of kind? Is Whitehead's God available for religious devotion? Hartshorne, Loomer, Niebuhr, and Thornton answer, "Yes"; Wieman and Temple, "Yes and No"; Lippman and Ely, "No."

Despite the lack of coherence among process theologians, process theology carries forward a most valuable underpinning for any christological prescription arising from the crossroads situation: the philosophical assumption most deeply resonant with the modern experience of reality—that change seems to be the only constant in the universe.

A Critique of Eschatological Theology

Pannenberg's assertion that the central meaning of the life, death, and resurrection of Jesus Christ lies in its eschatological function (the anticipation of God's future) suffers from the erosion of the passage of nearly two thousand years. Assuming, with Pannenberg, that the historicity and confirmatory nature of the resurrection did validate Jesus' proclamation of the coming kingdom of God, the modern honestly asks, If not by now, when? The passage of each year strains the waiting Christian's credibility more. The net effect is the dulling of the eschatological sensitivity of even those who appreciate Pannenberg's effort to build his Christology "from below." A further difficulty lies in the presupposition of Israel's election by God to special status, as seen and developed in Part I of this study.

The contribution of eschatological theology to a Christology for the crossroads situation, however, is great. It does focus attention in the necessary direction for a world facing an either/or choice and its consequences—the future.

A Critique of Death-of-God Theology

Even the boldest of the death-of-God theologians, Thomas J. J. Altizer, did not go far enough to speak fully christologically to the crossroads situation. He perceived and announced the ultimate incredibility for modern humanity of God as a Being-out-there, but concretized (literally kept alive that which he had just pronounced dead) that ultimate incredibility in Jesus Christ. To speak of the death of God as having taken place in Christ is to infer that God once lived; in effect, that the incredible was once credible. This is true enough in humanity's consciousness of the ultimate, *up to a point just short of the crossroads situation.* For those whose consciousness intuitively enables them to perceive the crossroads, there is no turning back; no acknowledgment possible that God as a Being-out-there ever was truly credible.

Death-of-God theology's gift to a Christology for the crossroads situation is its perception that with Christ, something very important died, even though it was not God.

A Critique of the Theology of Juxtaposition

Harvey Cox, with his image of Christ as harlequin, has presented a more adequate Christology for the crossroads

CONSCIOUSNESS AND THE ULTIMATE

situation than any other theologian discussed. Indeed, the pathos, weakness, and irony of a harlequinesque Christ does begin to make a strange kind of sense again, but in a new way, perceptible only in light of the new situation and only by those with a certain intuitive grasp. Cox has approached the threshold of a christological prescription for the consciousness of the ultimate, in light of the crossroads situation.

CHAPTER 18

THE WORLD D BOON: A CHRISTOLOGICAL PRESCRIPTION

A Recapitulation

The christological survey and critique have provided dimensions for a Christology with which Christian theology can speak meaningfully and forcefully to the crossroads situation—at least to those who are able to hear intuitively. From orthodoxy comes the assumption that the Christ-event was a once-and-for-all pivotal event in human history. From kenotic theory comes the feature of emptying—something precious was poured out. From liberalism comes the necessity for social action in response to that pivotal, emptying event. From neo-orthodoxy comes the force of a saving Word that was expressed somehow therein. From the theology of culture comes the element of newness. From process theology comes a philosophical basis—becoming, as opposed to being. From eschatological theology comes the focus in time—the future. From death-of-God theology comes the realization that something very important died with Christ. From the theology of juxtaposition comes the image needed for the christological prescription—Christ as harlequin.

A Parable

Once upon a time, there lived an emperor who did not care for soldiers or for the theater; he cared only for clothes, and he loved to walk through the town and show off his new clothes. He had a costume for every hour of the day.

Among the many who came to visit this happy land were two confidence men who claimed they knew how to manufacture beautiful cloth that had the amazing quality of becoming invisible to anyone who was not fit for his office or who was unpardonably stupid. The emperor gave the men money to begin weaving this wonderful material into a new suit. Each official who was sent to check on the progress of the work, believing himself not stupid, and not wanting to show himself unfit for office, pretended to see the nonexistent cloth. After hearing many glowing reports from his ministers, the emperor went to see for himself and solved the problem as had his emissaries: He went along with the "con."

At last the new clothes were ready, according to the wily weavers. So the emperor removed his clothes and was fitted with the various nonarticles—nonbreeches, noncoat, noncloak. Then he went for a stroll to show off his new clothes and proceeded down the avenue under the canopy carried by his admiring courtiers, while the people lined both sides of the street and expressed lavish praise. Except for one little child, who said, "He has nothing on!"

A Radical Christology

The Christology in light of the crossroads situation, perceptible to an intuitive few, is radical in the same sense as the observation by the little child about his naked emperor. Jesus the Christ is a cosmic joke, an essentially harlequinesque figure, the ultimate absurd fool, in that his (or his followers') is the most absurd claim to objectification of that which cannot be objectified.

Christ as harlequin is indeed a once-and-for-all pivotal historical event in the sense that before he came, it was possible to credibly personify ultimacy; afterward, there is no further possibility of its credible personification.

In Christ as harlequin, something indeed precious was emptied out: The intuitive few now can consciously "see" that ultimacy was thereby forever freed from the limiting (if devotion-inspiring) bonds of personification; freed from any form of meaningful objectification.

Christ as harlequin indeed requires a particular social action in response to his true nature: the shifting of conscious efforts from cultus (God-talk, things sacred, etc.) toward the attainment of unity-in-diversity at every level of human interaction, from one-to-one to humanity at large.

Indeed a saving Word is somehow expressed in Christ as harlequin, especially as salvation is related to expediting the movement toward the state of unity-in-diversity: Now it is forever clear that no one—priest, preacher, emperor, charismatic, or anyone—has special access to ultimacy; all humanity stands equal and is potentially "cremated equal" if unity-in-adversity fails to occur.

Indeed something new takes place in Christ as harlequin: The irreversible breakdown of legitimate distinctions between sacred and secular, heaven and earth, God and humanity, saved and lost, us and them, Christian and pagan, leaves only the two categories—the creative path (that which leads toward unity-in-diversity) and the destructive path (that which leads away from unity-in-diversity).

Indeed at last, in Christ as harlequin, "becoming" replaces "being" as the condition undergirding and emcompassing the two paths—creative and destructive; process replaces the idea of changelessness as a more apt description of things as they really are; the Clown points up the absurdity of the present situation, opening the way for creative becoming.

Christ as harlequin thereby indeed focuses, with regard to time, upon the future, upon the inbreaking eschaton, upon the crossroads choices and their creative or destructive implications for our children's children.

Indeed, in Christ as harlequin, something important died—any further opportunity for credible personification of the ultimate.

A Prescription

Christ as harlequin, then, for at least an intuitive few, personifies that which it is no longer possible (in light of the crossroads situation) to personify, and is therefore an absurd figure. This discovery by the intuitive of the deepest meaning of the Christ-event marks the final sweeping victory of the secularization process begun with the Renaissance challenge to Christendom. With this new awareness of the death of the specifically sacred, the intuitive at the same time realize the resurrection (from the long-ago time of the primitive, trusting, "dreaming"—Bellah's everywhen) of the generally awesome.

Thus the intuitive need no longer consciously invest psychic energy in the ultimate via the traditional so-called religious modalities. Furthermore, the intuitive, as citizens of World D, have a focus for this newly freed energy: the definition and elaboration of Unity-in-Diversity (now capitalized, a step toward its crystallization) in such a way as to lure those whose most highly developed mental function is other than intuition—citizens of Worlds C (thinking), B (feeling), and A (sensation)—onto the creative path toward Unity-in-Diversity. How? In part by assuming the harlequinesque role of jester.

The philosophy of the jester is a philosophy which in every epoch denounces as doubtful what appears as unshakable; it points out the contradictions in what seems evident and incontestable; it ridicules common sense into the absurd—in other words, it undertakes the daily toil of the jester's profession along with the inevitable risk of appearing ludicrous.[1]

World D Illuminative Case: The Church of Jesus Christ the Kidnapped

In his novel *Slapstick*, Kurt Vonnegut's protagonist, the final President of the United States, describes his discovery of the tiny Chicago cult destined to become the most popular American religion of all time, The Church of Jesus Christ the Kidnapped. While crossing a hotel lobby, he was handed a leaflet by "a clean and radical youth."

He was jerking his head around in what then seemed an eccentric manner, as though hoping to catch someone peering out at him from behind a potted palm tree or an easy chair, or even from

A CHRISTOLOGICAL PRESCRIPTION

directly overhead, from the crystal chandelier. . . .
"May I ask you what you're looking for, young man?" I said. "For our Saviour, sir," he replied. "You think He's in this hotel?" I said. "Read the leaflet, sir," he said.[2]

He did. Under a primitive picture of a tearful Jesus, gagged, handcuffed, and shackled, he found a catechism of questions and answers.

QUESTION: What is your name?
ANSWER: I am the Right Reverend William Uranium-8 Wainwright, founder of the Church of Jesus Christ the Kidnapped at 3972 Ellis Avenue, Chicago, Illinois.
QUESTION: When will God send us His Son again?
ANSWER: He already has. Jesus is here among us.
QUESTION: Why haven't we seen or heard anything about Him?
ANSWER: He has been kidnapped by the Forces of Evil.
QUESTION: What must we do?
ANSWER: We must drop whatever we are doing, and spend every waking hour in trying to find Him. If we do not, God will exercise His Option.
QUESTION: What is God's Option?
ANSWER: He can destroy Mankind so easily, any time He chooses to.[3]

The President saw the young man that evening eating alone in the dining room, and marveled that "he could jerk his head around and still eat without spilling a drop. He even looked under his plate and water glass for Jesus not once but over and over again. I had to laugh."

CHAPTER 19

THE PRESCRIPTION APPLIED TO WORLD C: FRAGMENTS FOR A HARLEQUINESQUE SYSTEMATIC THEOLOGY

Jesus Christ as Ultimate Harlequin

Some harlequinesque aspects of the person of Jesus Christ in the New Testament tradition have already been cited: Christ the King, riding a donkey; wearing a royal robe and a crown of thorns before his executioners. There are others: the inscription on the cross (King of the Jews); the awareness of Paul that his teachings are as foolishness to the wise (I Cor. 1:18-27); that those who follow Christ are in a sense fools (I Cor. 4:10); that if Christ be not risen, such preaching and faith therein is in vain (*fool*ish?) (I Cor. 15:14).

But a systematic theology centered upon Jesus Christ as harlequin does not assume its authority from the intriguing but rather tenuous thread of New Testament references. There is no conscious claim to the centrality of the harlequinesque image and idea in the New Testament, either by Jesus Christ or by his followers. The authority for the claim that the deepest meaning of the Christ-event lies in its decisive absurdity as the last attempt in human history to credibly personify ultimacy, arises from and is possible only in the midst of the current crossroads situation, as understood through the intuition of a few.

As indicated in the previous chapter, the image of Christ as harlequin most aptly conveys the simple, awesome truth, which humanity's religious consciousness now allows to be brought to bear: Personification (objectification) has been nothing more or less than an unconscious mechanism of the

PRESCRIPTION APPLIED TO WORLD C

mind, which seeks a way (the way of analogy) to conceptualize the subjective mysteries of ultimacy. (One must relate to persons every day; therefore, one somehow can relate to ultimacy if it is a He or a She—a Person or Persons, with a capital P.)

Furthermore, the image of Christ as Ultimate Harlequin serves as a collecting point for the best aspects of the Christologies formulated in ever-heightening consciousness of the ultimate. Thus the Incarnation remains the watershed historical event as lifted up by orthodoxy: Humanity can never again credibly personify ultimacy. It continues to affirm, with kenotic theory, that something precious was poured out: Ultimacy was forever freed from the limits of objectification. It focuses the essence of the social gospel—a course of social action designed to achieve Unity-in-Diversity at every level of human interaction: The process of ever-greater consciousness of the ultimate thereby becomes closely correlated with movement toward Unity-in-Diversity. It expresses a saving Word, the neo-orthodox concern, especially related to the way to move toward Unity-in-Diversity: Each human being has equal authority and responsibility with regard to consciousness of the ultimate in the movement toward achievement of Unity-in-Diversity. It introduces a new ingredient, if not the New Being: the emergence from the old broken dichotomous categories of sacred/secular, heaven/earth, God/humanity, saved/lost, us/them, and Christian/pagan, of only two viable categories—that which leads toward Unity-in-Diversity, the creative path; and that which leads away from Unity-in-Diversity, the destructive path. The only remaining meaningful categories emerge as pro- and anti-Unity-in-Diversity. It accepts process theology's philosophical base as more adequate than those of all previous theologies: The dynamic is given greater credence than the static. "Becoming" more aptly describes the true nature of the universe than does "being"; ultimacy is seen as at least partly in process. It identifies the future as the time in which Unity-in-Diversity will or will not be attained: The ultimate is not yet fully conscious. It signals the death of any further opportunity for credible personification of ultimacy: Ultimacy in personal form is no longer credible. It provides an absurd image to discredit all imagery with regard to ultimacy: Ultimacy must be sought consciously, without the use of imagery, other than that acknowledged as absurd.

God as Unity-in-Diversity-Plus

The cluster of meanings comprising the doctrine of Jesus Christ as Ultimate Harlequin impacts any credible, creative understanding of God in several ways.

First, attempts at meaningful use of the word God must be discontinued, since it is no longer possible to credibly personify ultimacy, and since God connotes not only the personal—a being—but even a male being. Here harlequinesque systematic theology joins forces with the so-called theologians of liberation, who clamor for an end to projections onto the word God of the particular racial, sexual, or even socioeconomic qualities of the one who happens to be speaking.[1] Harlequinesque theology also finds allies among the empiricist linguistic philosophers, who conclude that all theological talk about God has become meaningless.[2]

Second, since the consciousness of the ultimate is a continuing and deep human need, words or concept-phrases inevitably will rush in to fill the vacuum created by abandonment of the use of the word God. Harlinquinesque theology offers the concept-phrase Unity-in-Diversity-Plus as a meaningful replacement for the word God. Unity-in-Diversity-Plus is operationally defined as the ultimate concentration of consciousness in which each particular consciousness becomes still more itself.[3] This is the result of the principle of concretion having successfully invited movement "toward a definite outcome from an indeterminate situation," such principle being understood as a panentheistic inclusion of Creation, and more.[4] "Plus" is included to point up specifically the "and more," the final inability of this attempt at definition of that which is ultimately beyond adequate definition.

With regard to whether such Unity-in-Diversity-Plus merits devotion, Teilhard's words seem fitting: ". . . There is less difference than people think between research and adoration."[5]

Third, care needs to be taken *not* to project a harlequin image onto Unity-in-Diversity-Plus, lest in the very attempt to depersonify and thus better see Unity-in-Diversity-Plus as free, a new anthropomorphism (God as Harlequin) be created to replace the old (God the Father). No easy task, since with Melville's Ishmael in *Moby Dick*, one can easily muse about certain moments,

> when a man takes this whole universe for a vast practical joke, though the wit thereof he but dimly discerns, and more than suspects that the joke is at nobody's expense but his own.... And as for small difficulties and worryings, prospects of sudden disaster, peril of life and limb; all these, and death itself, seem to him only shy, good-natured hits, and jolly punches in the side bestowed by an unseen and unaccountable old joker.

Holy Spirit as Lure to Creative Emergence

In a harlequinesque doctrine of the Holy Spirit, dove and cloven-tongues-of-fire imagery give way to a phrase borrowed from Whitehead, "lure to creative emergence,"[6] accompanied by several associations.

The first association has to do with creativity. Less the highest of goods (Nietzsche) and more a unified intensity of feeling (Whitehead); not so much a life force (Bergson) as "the organic union of those factors which occur or can occur in creative action, and have a bearing on the production of creatures," creativity depends on power ("indeterminate intensity which tends as immanent causal ground toward change") as its primary term and depends on created form ("a consequent and dependent... novel in the sense that it has a beginning in time... [and] cannot be... analytically deduced") as its secondary term.[7]

The second association relates to negative entropy. Physics' second law of thermodynamics, also known as the law of entropy, states that any spontaneous changes in a physical system occur in the direction of increasing disorder; the final state of equilibrium corresponds to the maximum possible disarray. Transformation from simple to complex molecules, from chaos to ever-more-conscious life-forms, implies the *decrease* of entropy (disorder). Scientists point out the reason for this seeming contradiction: Rays of sunlight carry with them negative (actually low-level) entropy, which disappears when absorbed by green leaves; thus "the sun's radiation is robbed of the internal order with which it arrives on the earth, and this order is communicated to the molecules, permitting them to be built up into more complex, more orderly, configurations."[8]

The third association involves radial energy. In his attempts to avoid a fundamental dualistic division of the stuff of the universe into mind energy (the within), and matter energy (the without), Teilhard conceptualizes *all* energy as having two components. One is tangential and links an element with all others of the same order as itself. The other is radial, defined as that "which draws it towards ever greater complexity and centricity—in other words forwards." The course of movement by this radial energy is more easily backtracked into the past than projected into the future. How can this pathway be identified? Teilhard holds that this something that is jerkily but ceaselessly carried over on an axis, beginning in the earth itself and extending through the ever-more-complex life-forms in a rise of consciousness, can be plotted upward rather simply by the differentiation of nervous tissue—that is, by the development of the brain.[9]

Humanity as Conscious, Creative Creature

In the preface to this study the term "consciousness" was defined only tentatively as intending to delineate distinctly religious efforts without excluding the unconscious religious implications of secular activity. In a harlequinesque fragment on the doctrine of humanity, the term consciousness becomes one of three catchwords that attempt to capture the essence of homo sapiens. A more precise definition is required.

Consciousness . . . is a continuously unrolling, continuously developing activity of minds/brains in interaction with their environment, modified, either temporarily or permanently, by changing circumstances. . . . At any point in an individual's life-history, consciousness is an expression of the totality of his or her mind/brain activity in interaction with the environment. . . .

Furthermore, the degree of consciousness of an organism is some function of neuronal cell number and connectivity, perhaps of neurons of a particular type in association cortex regions. This function is of a threshold type such that there is a significant quantitative break with the emergence of humans.[10]

In this threshold phenomenon, Rose sees several humanizing factors involved: a somewhat larger brain in proportion to body weight; hand structure conducive to the manipulation of tools; vocal chords capable of clear articulation and the accompanying capacity to live in social groups; foreknowledge; a composite effect of the above factors in an increasing ability to control the natural world.

The second catchword is "creative." Humanity stands on the cutting edge of creativity by virtue of homo sapiens' position at the apex of the evolutionary process. In the physical sense, humans carry creative potential in their very loins; human sexuality is the capacity to transmit life in its most highly evolved form (on this planet, at least) into the future. In the mental sense, humans carry creative potential in their very brains; so far great strides have been made in realizing that potential: reshaping the conditions of life, changing the face of nature, eliminating killing disease, reconstructing the human body, controlling population growth, exploring the far universe, lengthening the life span, discovering energy sources, and cracking the genetic code.[11] To the extent that humanity can be said to be realizing its creative potential, human beings are indeed responding to the lure to Creative Emergence (harlequinesque Holy Spirit) on the path toward Unity-in-Diversity (which, when the Mystery-honoring word Plus is added, becomes the harlequinesque replacement phrase for the word God).

The third catchword, creature, is the result of creativity. Humanity is creature, inasmuch as homo sapiens meets the criteria by which creatures are delineated: having a beginning in time; having novelty, in that the creature "has a character which cannot be derived from the characters of other beings by a process of repetition, addition, and rearrangement"; and having form—"a determinate and unified character: a character limited in nature and distinguishable from other characters, and united within its boundary by homogeneity or more complex principles of union."[12]

Sin/Redemption as Movement Away From, or Toward, Unity-in-Diversity

Only two viable categories stand in the light of the consciousness of Jesus Christ as Ultimate Harlequin: that which leads toward Unity-in-Diversity (the creative path); and that which leads away from Unity-in-Diversity (the destructive path).

Thus sin, as deviation from the right way—as rebellion against a superior or unfaithfulness to an agreement (Old Testament); as lack of faith in Jesus Christ (New Testament); as having its locus in pride, very often most clearly expressed in sexuality (orthodoxy); as isolation from other humans and the universe (liberation); as a flaw in character inherited from Adam, causing humans to be born guilty (fundamentalism); and as the result of free choice (neo-orthodoxy)—all these meanings pale in the crossroads situation.

Also beginning to fade are their counterparts regarding redemption—as payment for that which is delivered (Old Testament); as ransom that cleanses from sin (New Testament); as involving God's free gift of grace (orthodoxy); as occurring in Jesus Christ the mediator (liberalism); as taking place via Jesus Christ's substitutionary atoning death (fundamentalism); and as reemphasis upon Jesus Christ the mediator by way of grace (neo-orthodoxy).

In harlequinesque theology, *sin* is both the mental state and any act resulting from a mind-set that *blocks, delays,* or in any way *deters* free communication and cooperation among persons, families, neighborhoods, communities, counties, states, and nations, with regard to the actualization and maintenance of an irreducible minimum of the psychological traits and aspirations that are the common possession of all humankind: to live, to be free, to express culturally affirmed values and to develop personally according to those values, to have power, and to achieve social distinctions—all attainable under similar world conditions involving proper management of plant and animal populations.

Conversely, in harlequinesque theology, *redemption* is the process that *enhances* free communication and cooperation among persons, families, neighborhoods, communities, counties, states, and nations, with regard to the actualization and maintenance of an irreducible minimum of the psychological traits and aspirations that are the common possession of all humankind: to live, to be free, to express (and to develop personally according to culturally affirmed values) to have power, and to achieve social distinctions—all attainable under similar world conditions involving proper management of plant and animal populations.

The goal toward which the redemptive process moves, against the resistance of sin, is Unity-in-Diversity.

Eschatology as Arrival at Unity-in-Diversity

Eschatology, the doctrine of last things, is most easily caricatured in its concrete, literal form prior to humanity's arrival at a harlequinesque Christian consciousness, in the following paragraph.

The Kingdom of God, the perfect society, awaits the Second Coming of Christ, when he will return upon the clouds and when history will end in catastrophe. Christ, having judged the living and the risen dead, will set up his Kingdom and rule for a thousand years, the millennium. At the end of that period there will be a final battle between the forces of God and Satan, and in the victory of God all the saints will be elevated to heaven for eternity while the damned will writhe in Hell.[13]

In light of the harlequinesque Christian consciousness, eschatology sheds its previous meanings in deference to a more Teilhardian imagery—arrival at Unity-in-Diversity, earlier defined as the ultimate concentration of consciousness.

CONSCIOUSNESS AND THE ULTIMATE

Teilhard's phrase is Omega Point—". . . a grouping in which personalisation of the All and personalisations of the elements reach their maximum, simultaneously and without merging, under the influence of a supremely autonomous focus of union."[14]

Unity-in-Diversity differs from Omega Point only in the omission of speculation about the "personalization of the All" and in the degree to which arrival there is seen as likely. Whereas Teilhard indicates that eventual arrival at the Omega Point is inevitable, arrival at Unity-in-Diversity depends upon the ability of humankind to discern and expedite certain courses of action, to be discussed in more detail in chapter 21.

World C Illuminative Case: Bokononism

This chapter heading contains the word "fragments," very carefully chosen to further convey the idea that at the level of consciousness now attained by humankind, it is no longer possible to credibly objectify, personify, or even systematize ultimacy. The heading is even a contradiction in terms since it links harlequinesque theology (meaning the absurdity of all attempts to credibly objectify ultimacy) with systematic theology. So be it.

Given such a paradox, any religious system attempting to seriously consider the now-conscious harlequinesque quality of all attempts to credibly objectify ultimacy, must declare its intentions from the outset.

One example of such a harlequinesque systematic theology is to be found in the fertile writings of Kurt Vonnegut, Jr. *Cat's Cradle* is a story about the end of the world. Most of the action takes place on the tiny Caribbean isle of San Lorenzo, discovered in 1922 by a black World War I veteran, Lionel Boyd Johnson, and a white United States Marine deserter, Corporal Earl McCabe. Shipwrecked, they are washed ashore stark naked. Adventurers both, Johnson and McCabe successfully wrench the listless inhabitants from the grip of a large sugar company and decide to turn the island into a utopia.

PRESCRIPTION APPLIED TO WORLD C

McCabe takes over the government, and Johnson (Bokonon, in native phonetics) invents a new religion. When it becomes clear that no reform can bring relief to the destitute people, Bokonon asks McCabe to outlaw him and his religion (now universally practiced on San Lorenzo) in order to put some zest into life on the impoverished island.

> So I said good-bye to government,
> And I gave my reason:
> That a really good religion
> Is a form of treason.[15]

Life remains as grim and brief as ever, but the people find increasing happiness as McCabe acts out his role of cruel tyrant and Bokonon, that of banished holy man. The nature and purpose of Bokononism is capsuled in this calypso from "The Books of Bokonon":

> I wanted all things
> To seem to make some sense,
> So we all could be happy, yes,
> Instead of tense.
> And I made up lies
> So that they all fit nice,
> And I made this sad world
> A par-a-dise.[16]

Bokonon pulls no punches. The first sentence in "The Books of Bokonon" is this: "All of the true things I am about to tell you are shameless lies." On the title page of the first book appears the warning, "Don't be a fool! Close this book at once! It is nothing but *foma* [harmless untruths]!" Again, in "The Books of Bokonon" (1:5) are the words, "Live by the *foma* that make you brave and kind and healthy and happy."[17] And so San Lorenzans do, with considerable improvement in the quality of their lives. These are some of the Bokononist concepts.

karass: Humanity . . . organized into teams . . . that do God's will without ever discovering what they are doing.

vin-dit: A sudden, very personal shove in the direction of believing that . . . God Almighty has some pretty elaborate plans for [one].

CONSCIOUSNESS AND THE ULTIMATE

granfalloon: A false *karass* . . . a seeming team . . . meaningless in terms of the ways God gets things done.[18]

Examples of *granfalloons* are Hoosiers, the Communist Party, the D.A.R., corporations, and nations. And religions.

CHAPTER 20

THE PRESCRIPTION APPLIED TO WORLD B: HARLEQUINESQUE PASTORAL CARE

Introductory Comment

Systems, diagnostic schemes, and even religious beliefs come and go, but human beings continue to experience suffering as a part of their very human condition. From the trauma of birth to the last raspy breath before death, each developmental stage in life brings unique opportunity and difficulty. In addition, natural and human-induced disasters remain a constant danger. Loss of significant goals and persons are potentially ever present. These components of the human situation are equally real for all people, whether their most highly developed mental function is sensation, feeling, thinking, or intuition.

In such crises, citizens of Worlds A, B, C, and D, in varying degrees of awareness, find themselves undergoing emotional distress, a phenomenon normally associated with feeling-dominant World B. As described in chapter 13, the theological subdiscipline, known variously as spiritual guidance, the cure of souls, and pastoral care, concerns itself with attempts to assist the distressed person.

Harlequinesque pastoral care—pastoral care that reflects consciousness of the Christ-event as the decisive absurdity, the last attempt in human history to credibly personify (objectify) ultimacy—is uniquely capable of sensitively responding to distressed persons in any of the worlds in an appropriate way, since it is the first pastoral care to identify and consider the characteristics of the four worlds.[1]

CONSCIOUSNESS AND THE ULTIMATE

Harlequinesque Pastoral Care for the World A Citizen

What would have been harlequinesque pastoral care for the widow in chapter 12, who so stoically took her suffering as a matter of course? The chaplain would have had no need to challenge her directly when she said, "I guess that I was supposed to go through these things or I would not have had to." He would have been more comfortable with the language of myth, less threatened by her peacefulness, more perceptive, and more respectful of her spiritual state.

An individual living in World A simply accepts things as they are and therefore, in a sense, is not ready for any meaningful authoritative intervention. When the chaplain moved to exercise a World B kind of authority ("Well, I don't feel that way"), she was not only not open to it, but became defensive ("Well, the Lord has seen me through, hasn't he?").

John T. McNeill aptly points out, in his classic survey *A History of the Cure of Souls*, that pastoral care "is never merely a method, even a method derived from a doctrine, or a task for certain hours in the week, but that it involves both the faith we live by and all our daily activities and contacts." Yet he does find significant differences among pastors down through the centuries in their exercise of authority and asks, "To what degree should [the pastoral] relationship involve the authority of the [guide] over the [guided person]?"[2]

Harlequinesque pastoral care answers McNeill with a generalization.

> With regard to the exercise of pastoral authority, pastoral care to a World A person is best expressed in passive being-with.[3]

Harlequinesque Pastoral Care for the World B Citizen

What would have been harlequinesque pastoral care for the woman stalled in labor, described in chapter 13, who turned her problem over to an acknowledged authority with sacred qualities—the chaplain?

Precisely what the chaplain did in this case. He perceived her World B need rather easily. A citizen of World C himself, he was able to step into World B just long enough to respond to her on her terms, using what for him was a broken symbol (prayer), but for her was a literal symbol.

Concerning McNeill's question about the degree of authority to be used, harlequinesque pastoral care answers with a second generalization.

> With regard to the exercise of pastoral authority, pastoral care to a World B person is best expressed in active doing-for.[4]

Harlequinesque Pastoral Care for the World C Citizen

What would have been harlequinesque pastoral care for the young couple in chapter 14, whose newborn twins were in jeopardy and who asked that the babies be baptized?

Again, precisely what the chaplain did in this case, though it caused him considerable anxiety and actually precipitated his own arrival in World C. As noted earlier, after the baptisms had taken place the chaplain discovered the parents' request had not come out of their own religious convictions (a World C-like respectful skepticism, in which baptism was a broken symbol). The parents had sought the baptisms to ease the minds of *their* parents (solid citizens of World B, for whom baptism was very much a literal symbol).

McNeill's question about the degree of authority to be used, when applied by harlequinesque pastoral care, yields a third generalization.

> With regard to the exercise of pastoral authority, pastoral care to a World C person is best expressed in peerish give-and-take.[5]

Harlequinesque Pastoral Care for the World D Citizen

What would have been harlequinesque pastoral care for the divorcee described in chapter 15, who experienced sleeplessness and weight loss in the midst of her quest?

Precisely what her parents did in this case: They took her home, and while ministering to her physical needs, stood beside her emotionally, resisting any impulses they may have had to chastize her or to offer advice.

Since World D intuition and World A sensation are the two mental functions seen by Jung as primarily unconscious-rooted, the generalized answer to McNeill's question about the exercise of pastoral authority is the same for both World D and World A harlequinesque pastoral care.

> With regard to the exercise of pastoral authority, pastoral care to a World D person is best expressed in passive being-with.[6]

World B Illuminative Case: People's Temple

A gross example of World B pastoral care at its worst—of active doing-for carried to its tragic extreme—is the case of The Reverend Jim Jones and the People's Temple.[7]

James Warren Jones was born in 1931, the only child of a disabled World War I veteran, in Lynn, Indiana. His mother, dark of complexion (possibly part Cherokee) and much younger than her husband, was thought to be somewhat odd by the townsfolk—she cursed with proficiency, kept to herself—and gained notoriety as the first woman to stroll down the street smoking a cigarette. She was a factory worker, and the father, though active in the local Ku Klux Klan, spent most of his time indoors due to ill health. Thus Jim received minimal parental supervision, growing up on the streets.

He was influenced religiously by a neighbor who introduced him to the Nazarene faith, and later he drifted freely in and out of Lynn's six churches. By high school age, Jim was known as an average student with a bad temper, a growing sense of racial injustice, and a certain charismatic air. Upon graduation in 1949, he entered Indiana University while seriously considering the ministry as a career. He dropped out, took a job in a Richmond hospital, and soon met and married Marceline, a nurse and "mother figure" four years his senior.

In 1950 Jones became a pastor at Sommerset Southside Church in Indianapolis, also taking over and operating an integrated community center. Angered by resistance there to his liberal view on civil rights, he broke away and founded the Community Unity Church in another Indianapolis neighborhood. There he sought to make his dream of building a racially integrated congregation come true.

By 1956 he had opened the People's Temple in a section of the city in transition from white to black and refined his leadership style in the mold of Philadelphia's authoritarian Father Divine, as exemplified by the creation of an interrogation committee charged with disciplining anyone who spoke against him. Discipline ranged from verbal abuse to actual physical beating.

In the meantime his family had expanded to include seven adopted children of black, white, and Asian extraction. In 1960 Mayor Charles Boswell appointed Jim Jones director of the Indianapolis Human Rights Commission, a post which generated strong antagonism. "For three solid months, segregationists tossed rocks at his home, called him on the phone, demanding, 'Niggerlover, get out of town,' and threw explosives into his yard."

Jones' embattled congregation grew. By 1963, now known as the People's Temple Full Gospel Church (Disciples of Christ), it claimed to be serving more than one thousand free meals a week to needy persons. At the height of the racially induced struggle, Jim Jones "experienced a 'personal vision' of a coming nuclear holocaust that would poison the world."

The next two years were characterized by three themes. First, Jones seemed to be on the lookout for a relocation site relatively safe from atomic attack. Second, he placed great emphasis on controversial healing miracles, using patterns practiced by Father Divine. Third, he experienced increasing financial difficulties, accompanied by scrutiny from the Indiana Secretary of State and the federal Internal Revenue Service. Thus, in mid-1965 some 150 members moved with him to reestablish the People's Temple in Ukiah, California, 116 miles north of San Francisco. The congregation grew to

300 by 1967, and once more came under attack for its strong stand for racial equality.

Again restless, Jones bought an auditorium in San Francisco in 1972 and moved his headquarters there. Through spectacular staged healing services and continued political activism, Jones became a real force on the San Francisco scene. Eight hundred People's Temple members worked to get out the vote for mayoral candidate George Moscone in 1975. Moscone enjoyed a twelve-to-one margin of victory in some precincts and later helped Jones obtain the chairmanship of the local housing authority.

How did Jones weld his followers into such a disciplined force? By taking total responsibility for their welfare and, in turn, demanding their total allegiance. He took over members' social-security checks, property, and power of attorney. He used flattery, fear, guilt, sex, violence, and the cutting of family and personal ties (even among family units within the Temple) to enhance his role "as the only major figure in a member's life." He promised that no one who joined the Temple would ever die!

Using such tactics, Jones amassed property and funds to the tune of a $600,000 local annual budget and up to $1,000,000 per year to develop his utopian colony in Guyana, established in 1973—the so-called agricultural mission. Jonestown was to be his refuge against race war and nuclear holocaust. Smarting from the sting of magazine and newspaper articles critical of the spectacular healings and shady political and financial maneuvers of the People's Temple, in 1977 Jim Jones moved the bulk of the membership to Guyana.

And there the momentum, increased by the isolation itself and by the increasing paranoia within Jones, built toward its grisly climax: his claims to be the reincarnation of Lenin and Christ; rehearsals for mass suicide; the visit and death of Congressman Leo Ryan and four members of his party; the ingestion of cyanide-laced Kool-Aid by some 900 Temple members, and on November 18, 1978, the resulting mass death.

CHAPTER 21

THE PRESCRIPTION APPLIED TO WORLD A: HARLEQUINESQUE MISSIONS

Introductory Comment

World A—the arena of the five senses, the realm of the physical—is where the action is. Traditionally, the subdiscipline in theology most engaged in the activity of propagating the faith in the world in the actual, physical sense, is known as mission. Thus harlequinesque mission strategy and tactics come to the fore, particularly in the application of the prescription to World A. Christ the Ultimate Harlequin, the final attempt to credibly personify ultimacy and therefore the decisive absurdity, intuitively seen in the heightened consciousness of the historical crossroads situation, frees psychic energy from investment in traditional so-called religious modalities, to engage in luring citizens of all worlds onto the path toward Unity-in-Diversity.

Since in harlequinesque theology, sin is both the mental state and any act resulting from a mind-set that blocks, delays, or in any way deters free communication and cooperation among persons, families, neighborhoods, communities, counties, states, and nations, with regard to the actualization and maintenance of an irreducible minimum of psychological traits and aspirations; and since in harlequinesque theology, redemption is the process that enhances free communication and cooperation among persons, it follows that harlequinesque mission strategy must so clearly identify sinful forces and their effects that movement on the destructive path away from Unity-in-Diversity is halted and reversed. The method by which the strategy can be implemented grows out of the harlequinesque image itself—the role of jester: Denounce as doubtful what appears as unshakable; point out the contradictions in what seems evident and incontestable; ridicule common sense into the absurd.

In general, the target for harlequinesque mission strategy is elitism in its various forms, in light of the irreversible breakdown of legitimate distinctions between sacred and secular, heaven and earth, God and humanity, saved and lost, us and them, Christian and pagan. Specific tactics grow out of overall harlequinesque mission strategy in the battle against elitism in its specific forms in the political, demographic/ecological/economic, scientific, and religious spheres.

In the Political Sphere

What is the tactical target for harlequinesque missions' role of jester in the political sphere, in order to halt and reverse movement on the destructive path away from Unity-in-Diversity? Doctrinaire nationalism, especially as it stands in the way of increasing world harmony and peace.

"A Nation . . . is a group of persons united by a common error about their ancestry and a common dislike of their neighbors." Karl W. Deutsch has identified six integrative processes involved in the creation of the nations of western Europe: the development of countries (defined as "area(s) of markedly high interdependence"); the consolidation of language; the dominance of a particular social group whose behaviors, speech, and so on become the accepted standard (the "southern aristocracy" in the six counties around London, England, for example); the expansion of feelings of kinship, from actual tribal kinship to that of whole peoples and cultures; the development of common interests, unity, and trust within peoples; and the political integration of administrative districts.[1]

As already noted in the Part I discussion of intimacy in its political dimension, the human capacity for identification and therewith, the six-faceted integrative process described by Deutsch, seem to reach their limits at national boundary lines. Heilbroner's call for all peoples to form a collective bond of common identity with the generations of the future by identifying with our children's children, points toward harlequinesque redemption, yet seems uncomfortably vague.

What specific tactics can be employed to aid in the move toward such transnational identification? Denounce as doubtful, point out contradictions, and ridicule every instance of doctrinaire nationalistic elitism.

For example, in Part I, Judaism was characterized as less a personally founded religion (by Moses) than a monotheistic national identity emerging from tribal confederacy and polytheistic thought. Unaccounted for is the hatred and prejudice behind centuries of persecution, culminating in what has come to be known as the Holocaust, the Nazi murder of some nine million Jews. One explanation for the buildup of such genocidal rage is that it is in part the outsiders' reaction to the self-proclaimed insiders' claim that they are special, super, unique, chosen.

God made covenant with a particular people that it should be His priesthood. To this people, the seed of Abraham, the slaves He had just redeemed from Egypt, He revealed the Torah, the Law which they were to obey, as the particular burden of the Jews and as the sign of their unique destiny in the world. He chose the land of Canaan as His inheritance and that of His people, the Holy Land which would forever remain the place in which He would most clearly be manifest.[2]

The harlequinesque response? Turn the page!!

In the Demographic/Ecological/Economic Sphere

The tactical target for harlequinesque missions' jester role in the demographic/ecological/economic sphere, in order to halt and reverse movement on the destructive path away from Unity-in-Diversity, is growth/productivity per se, especially as it effectively widens the gap between the rich and the poor nations of the world.

CONSCIOUSNESS AND THE ULTIMATE

Oliphant, *The Washington Star*.

Visionaries since Matthew have raised their voices in warning against the combined effects of burgeoning world population and shrinking world resources; of amassed wealth by a few and increased poverty amidst the many. Part I treated intimacy in a summary separate from its worldwide implications—for example, in its demographic, ecological, and economic "dimensions." At this point the three areas are considered together. Why? At least for the United States,

> an increasing gross national product (GNP) has functioned in American society like a god-concept does in a religious society. In a word, Americans worship economic growth. Yet increased economic growth, which comes about by increased material and power consumption, is always accompanied by increased pollution. Hence, many ecologists and others believe that we must begin to deal with root causes, and not symptoms. And perpetually increasing consumption levels of power and material goods (compounded by the population explosion) are the root causes.[3]

To get at these root causes, Alvin Toffler calls for "public self-examination aimed at broadening and defining in social, as well as merely economic terms, the goals of 'progress.' "[4] Charles A. Reich pushes for what he labels Consciousness III, which "seeks restoration of the nonmaterial elements of man's existence, the elements like the natural environment and the spiritual that were passed by in the rush of material development."[5] Paul R. Ehrlich targets "a dramatic change in our idea of 'needs,' " requiring strict controls, since, backed by business, advertising often creates irrational needs based less on quality than on illusory differences between identical products.[6] The Club of Rome, the informal association of some one hundred leading international businessmen, which jolted the world in 1972 with its "no growth" message in *The Limits to Growth*, has moved to a selective-growth model, requiring "voluntary actions aimed at speeding the development of the poorer countries while slowing that of their industrialized brethren," in the cause of global prosperity through economic interdependence.[7]

All these efforts are within the harlequinesque tactical thrust: Denounce as doubtful, point out contradictions, and ridicule instances of the apotheosis of growth/productivity per se.

In the Scientific Sphere

The tactical target for harlequinesque missions' jester role in the scientific sphere, in order to halt and reverse movement on the path away from Unity-in-Diversity?—Specialization, especially as a value in and of itself.

To read the list of titles of doctoral dissertations on any university commencement program is to be jolted into sharp awareness of the degree to which scientific endeavor has become specialized and compartmentalized. John B. Cobb, Jr., has condemned this tendency as totally wrong, in that it substitutes knowledge for wisdom. The fragmentation experienced by the development of a science into increasingly esoteric subspecialties, as evidenced in the structure of universities and professions, does not allow for a wholistic vision and leads to such absurdities as the agribusiness "success" in Kenya. There the life of the land for cattle-grazing has been extended from ten to fifty years, when such use, in the overall picture, already has destroyed 50 percent of the earth's arable land.

In the true harlequinesque spirit, Cobb poses a solution to the problem that despite the rapid depletion of energy sources, American technology is still being applied to make more profits: Sell the sun to General Motors![8]

In the Religious Sphere

The tactical target for harlequinesque missions' jester role in the religious sphere, in order to halt and reverse movement on the destructive path away from Unity-in-Diversity is competition, expecially as it tends to reinforce the now meaningless distinctions between us/them. In this, the last section in the body of this work, it seems fitting to move past the more obvious possibilities for comment and ironic anecdote regarding the proliferation of religious cults, sects, and the mindless competition among endless variations thereof, to a positive example of movement on the path *toward* Unity-in-Diversity.

In 1956, the doors opened on a new medical center associated with a state university in a small midwestern college town.[9] Within a few months, local pastors had received so many requests from their peers in outlying areas that the local pastors visit the out-of-town parishioners who were hospitalized, the pastors approached the university administration in a group, to request that a chaplaincy program be started. Caution, combined with an especially stringent state constitutional sentence on church-state separation, produced a No.

But three or four of the pastors (each of a different Protestant denomination) developed a plan whereby an adjacent mental-health center agreed to provide one-half of a chaplain's salary in return for half his time; a not-for-profit corporation, funded by regular gifts from twelve different churches, of nine distinct denominations, agreed to provide the other half of the salary for services rendered in the medical center; and the university agreed to provide indirect costs, such as office space, secretarial support, and professional travel expenses.

From that complicated but modest beginning, the program has grown from a one-person-for-one-job ministry to an area-wide endeavor involving eighteen Protestant churches, the Catholic diocese, at least token support from the Jewish community, five area hospitals, two nursing homes, two crisis centers, visiting nurses, and the police. It utilizes the services of six paid staff ministers, several ministerial trainees, and a cadre of some forty local clergy and laity who serve in various ways as volunteers.

By concentrating on the common concern of ministering to human need and by minimizing their differences, a normally highly competitive group from the religious community has worked with equally competitive, even hostile, health-care institutions, to develop and maintain quality pastoral care services, and without a loss of identity as distinct units. Unity-in-Diversity! Plus!

EPILOGUE

The preface promised that the epilogue would offer a measure of the strengths and weaknesses of this study, using the eightfold standard of Isenberg and Owen to which the responsible methodology must answer, in terms of its ability to handle a complex set of interlocking problems.

According to Isenberg and Owen, the responsible methodology first must bridge the gap between the sociology of religion and the psychology of religion by considering equally the communal religious phenomena and the religious experiences of individuals.

Part I, "History," is, by definition, focused upon the sociological as it attempts to identify stages in the rising consciousness of the ultimate in human beings en masse. On the other hand, Part II, "Psychology," also by definition, is focused upon the psychological, as it attempts to recognize distinct categories within which the ultimate is variously consciously expressed by individual human beings. Furthermore, Part III, "Theology," is in part a synthesis, which draws equally on the history and the psychology of consciousness of the ultimate in moving toward conclusions. Thus this study registers a strong plus in terms of the first criterion.

Second, in the view of Isenberg and Owen, the classifications used in any responsible methodology should not carry inherent value judgments to the effect that it is better to be in one class than another—that it is inherently better to be modern, for example, than primitive. The eight major classifications within Part I were originally set forth by Erik Erikson in his attempts to better understand the individuals with whom he worked as an analyst. As developmental crisis categories, each with its own built-in desirable and undesirable resolutions, the system successfully evades the values trap. Who can be blamed for being a certain age at a certain time and therefore fitting into the appropriate developmental category described by Erikson as universally pertinent to those reaching a particular chronological age? Similarly, and for purposes of this study, who can reasonably be looked down upon for being born in 2000 B.C. instead of, say, A.D. 1500? Both time situations have their advantages, disadvantages, and unique developmental implications.

The four major classifications within Part II are those of Carl Jung who, as already noted, saw them as similar to the four points on the compass; they are equally as arbitrary and as indispensable. Again the values test is passed. Part III, however, *is* vulnerable to the charge that it is inherently better to be in one of its categories (the christological category of Christ the harlequin) than in any of the others, and therefore Part III fails to measure up to the second criterion.

The third requirement of Isenberg and Owen for a responsible methodology is that the system should be comprehensive enough to allow meaningful comparisons and differentiations across geographical and time lines. Part I ranges from the dawn of prehistory to the present, with speculations about the future; from a vaguely worldwide perspective, toward an admittedly more narrow Western view geographically. Part II sets forth a scheme of mind functions found currently in individual human beings all around the world. Part III, concluding as it does that consciousness of the ultimate now must occur in a world and an age where traditional distinctions between sacred and secular are no longer meaningful, has its basis in the very concerns of Isenberg and Owen's third requirement—

that meaningful comparisons and differentiations can be (and are herein) made across geographical and time lines.

For Isenberg and Owen, fourth, the effort should not be reductionist, *a priori*. On its face, this study may be seen as a direct breach of this criterion. Part I attempts to squeeze the vastly complex religious history of humankind into a simplistic eight-stage scheme (Erikson's eight ages of man) originally intended for use in the study of individual psychosocial development. True enough. Similar comments could be made for Parts II and III. However, the fourth requirement of Isenberg and Owen must not be taken to its extreme, where it would reinforce the *a priori* myth of Science with a capital S, as expressed in logical positivism and in the excesses of behaviorism. Values *do* enter into investigation as bias (a conclusion arrived at prior to the gathering of evidence and maintained independently of it), *but also and inevitably* as the very subject matter for investigation, as the ethics of the investigator, as a basis for the selection of problems, as determinants of the meanings seen in the subject matter, and as the determination of what constitutes a fact.[1] Furthermore, the establishment of exhaustive, mutually exclusive categories is essential to the development of any respectable, credible methodology, because such process facilitates breaking the problem down into more manageable (measurable), more discriminating, more differentiating, more discrete, more easily communicated components. None of the systems adapted to this study (Erikson's eight ages of man; Jung's four functions of the mind; Tillich's naturalism, repressed literalism, and broken myth; and Cox's harlequin) were clearly decided upon prior to the study. Rather, they were finally selected from among the many available models and schemes (with considerable apprehension about their limitations) as best able to communicate what had been discovered regarding consciousness of the ultimate.

Fifth, according to Isenberg and Owen, the responsible methodology should be able to adequately appreciate both the simple social setting of the tribe and the massive differentiation of the industrial society. Part I is largely the recounting, with particular focus on the impact upon

EPILOGUE

consciousness of the ultimate, of that very process—from tribe to town to nation to ever-shrinking world community. Parts II and III deal with its implications via psychology and theology.

Isenberg and Owen's sixth criterion—that the methodology should be flexible enough to absorb and appreciate the unexpected but inevitable defiantly unclassifiable schisms that come along—is not well met in this study. For example, the Reformation, that movement of profound consequence, receives only a parenthetical note of disclaimer in this study's section on the historical adolescence of Christianity.

The seventh feature of Isenberg and Owen's responsible methodology—that its theory should have the capability to generate empirically disconfirmable hypotheses—has yet to be tested. Possible hypotheses might include: Statistically significant numbers of female figurines with exaggerated sexual features have been unearthed from the period associated with the earliest development of agriculture in various parts of the world; the god-myths of nomadic tribes have a significantly greater number of features (personality traits) usually associated with masculinity, whereas the god-myths of agricultural societies have a significantly greater number of features (personality traits) usually associated with femininity; all seven men who founded lasting (living) world religions were born in the period 660 B.C.–A.D. 632; and so on.

The final criterion of Isenberg and Owen, that the methodology should be meaningful to and workable for both the personally religious and the authentically secular individual, seems to assume the two states to be mutually exclusive. On the contrary, it is the drive to integrate both, or at least to consider seriously and respectfully the interplay between both these realities within the same person, which brought this study into being in the first place.

NOTES

PREFACE

1. James Reston, "World Morality Crisis," *New York Times,* June 6, 1968.
2. Mircea Eliade, *The Quest* (Chicago: University of Chicago Press, 1969), p. 9.
3. Sheldon R. Isenberg and Dennis E. Owen, "Bodies, Natural and Contrived: The Work of Mary Douglas," *Religious Studies Review,* vol. 3 (January 1977), pp. 1-2.

CHAPTER 1. BEGINNINGS

1. Eliade, *Quest,* p. 25.
2. *Ibid.,* p. 50.
3. John B. Noss, *Man's Religions,* 5th ed. (New York: The Macmillan Co., 1974), pp. 3-7.
4. *Ibid.,* pp. 7-9.
5. Joseph Campbell, *The Masks of God: Primitive Mythology* (New York: Viking Press, 1969), pp. 138-39. To avoid oversimplification it should be noted that different parts of the world developed at different rates; the focus of this discussion is upon the Near East c. 5000 B.C. Further, some authorities hold that female fertility figurines appeared as long ago as 30,000 years.

CHAPTER 2. STAGE ONE: BASIC TRUST

1. John J. Gleason, Jr., *Growing Up to God* (Nashville: Abingdon Press, 1975), p. 26.
2. Campbell, *Primitive Mythology,* p. 139.
3. *Ibid.,* p. 71.
4. Violet S. deLaszlo, ed., *The Basic Writings of C. G. Jung* (New York: Random House, Modern Library, 1959), p. 287.
5. *Ibid.,* p. 289.

6. *Ibid.*, p. 327.
7. *Ibid.*, p. 333.
8. *Ibid.*, p. 335.
9. David M. Schneider and Kathleen Gough, eds., *Matrilineal Kinship* (Berkeley: University of California Press, 1961), p. vii.
10. *Ibid.*, p. xi.
11. *Ibid.*, pp. vii-xiii; Table 17-4 (cont.), p. 678.
12. Harvey Cox, *The Secular City* (New York: The Macmillan Co., 1965), p. 7.
13. *Ibid.*, p. 10.
14. Robert N. Bellah, *Beyond Belief* (New York: Harper & Row, 1970), pp. 20-50.
15. *Ibid.*, pp. 26-27.
16. *Ibid.*, pp. 28-29.
17. *Ibid.*, pp. 29, 30, 31.
18. Noss, *Man's Religions*, pp. 9-19.
19. Campbell, *Primitive Mythology*, p. 63.

CHAPTER 3. STAGE TWO: AUTONOMY

1. Gleason, *Growing*, pp. 38-40.
2. Joseph Campbell, *The Masks of God: Occidental Mythology* (New York: Viking Press, 1969), p. 72.
3. *Ibid.*, p. 73.
4. *Ibid.*, pp. 74-75.
5. *Ibid.*, pp. 75-76.
6. Raffaele Pettazoni, "The Supreme Being," *The History of Religions*, ed. Mircea Eliade and J. M. Kitagawa (Chicago: University of Chicago Press, 1959), pp. 64-66.
7. E. O. James, *The Worship of the Sky-God* (University of London: Athlone Press, 1963), p. 20.
8. *Ibid.*, pp. 1-30, 3, 4, 5, 9, 10-11, 11-12, 14, 31, 50.
9. Cox, *Secular City*, p. 10.
10. *Ibid.*, p. 12.
11. Bellah, *Beyond Belief*, pp. 29-32, 35.
12. Noss, *Man's Religions*, pp. 34-35, 51-77.
13. James, *Worship of Sky-God*, p. 49. The issue of whether Judaism is a personally founded (by Moses) world religion must be briefly examined because this factor is being used arbitrarily in this study as a criterion for entry of humanity into stage three, initiative/sin and redemption. James (pp. 50-51) holds that it is not really ascertainable from available data whether Yahweh of the Hebrew tradition was worshiped before the time of Moses. Yet James' reasoning is very convincing in the argument that Yahweh was not a totally new god at the time of Moses and that therefore Moses did not personally found Judaism in the same sense in which Zoroaster founded Zoroastrianism and Jesus founded Christianity. Moses' ability to motivate an enslaved people by invoking the name and powers of a completely unknown Yahweh is seen as highly unlikely. Additionally, the northern tribes, who were not with Moses at the time of the Exodus, did not ascribe the beginnings of their Yahweh allegiance to Moses. This study assumes, therefore, that the role of Moses in the development of the emerging

NOTES FOR PAGES 36–49

national religion of Israel, though creative in the highest sense, was primarily that of mobilizer and enabler, not founder.
14. *Ibid.*, p. 47, citing Genesis 12:6-7, 13:18, and 28:10-22.
15. W. F. Albright, *From the Stone Age to Christianity* (Baltimore: Johns Hopkins Press, 1940), pp. 187-88.
16. O. S. Rankin, "Names of God," *A Theological Word Book of the Bible*, ed. Alan Richardson (London: SCM Press, 1957), p. 94.
17. *Ibid.*, p. 95.
18. *Ibid.*, p. 96.

CHAPTER 4. STAGE THREE: INITIATIVE

1. For purposes of this study, Hinduism, Judaism, and Shintoism are considered to be national (not personally founded) lasting religions. Nanek (A.D. 1469–1538), founder of Sikhism, is not on the list because of the strongly syncretistic aspects of Sikhism.
2. Gleason, *Growing*, pp. 49-51.
3. Noss, *Man's Religions*, pp. 338-39.
4. A. V. Williams Jackson, *Zoroaster* (New York: AMS Press, 1965), pp. 307-8.
5. Noss, *Man's Religions*, p. 251.
6. Tao-Te Ching.
7. Noss, *Man's Religions*, pp. 107-13.
8. *Ibid.*, pp. 118-25.
9. "The Nine Incapabilities."
10. Noss, *Man's Religions*, pp. 271-78.
11. Mark 2:5-10.
12. Noss, *Man's Religions*, pp. 431-33.
13. Mark 14:36.
14. Noss, *Man's Religions*, pp. 511-14.
15. Ballou, Robert O., ed., *Portable World Bible* (New York: Viking Press, 1967), pp. 440-45.
16. Noss, *Man's Religions*, pp. 517-18.
17. No specific illuminative case is offered; it is hoped that the discussions of the seven lasting-religion founders provide sufficient illumination.

CHAPTER 5. STAGE FOUR: INDUSTRY

1. From this point forward the study is limited to a consideration of the developing religious consciousness in the West—i.e., Western civilization. Western culture in general and Western Christianity in particular now becomes and remains the ongoing illuminative case.
2. Mark 1:14-15.
3. Richardson, *Theological Word Book*, p. 119.
4. O. E. Evans, "Kingdom of God," *The Interpreter's Dictionary of the Bible*, vol. 2, ed. George A. Buttrick, *et al.* (New York/Nashville: Abingdon Press, 1962), p. 20.
5. Luke 17:20b-21.
6. Alan Wells, *Social Institutions* (New York: Basic Books, 1971), p. 258.
7. Hugh Anderson, *Jesus* (Englewood Cliffs, N.J.: Prentice-Hall, 1967), pp. 49-52.
8. Talcott Parsons, "Introduction," *The Sociology of Religion*, Max Weber, trans. Ephraim Fischoff (Boston: Beacon Press, 1963), p. xxxiii.

9. Eric Hoffer, *The True Believer* (New York: New American Library, 1958), p. 119.
10. Thomas F. O'Dea, "Five Dilemmas in the Institutionalization of Religion," *The Sociology of Religion, An Anthology*, ed. Richard D. Knudten (New York: Appleton-Century-Crofts, 1967), p. 285.
11. Acts 20:22-25.
12. A. C. Purdy, "Paul the Apostle," *The Interpreter's Dictionary of the Bible*, Buttrick, pp. 681-704.
13. Wells, *Social Institutions*, p. 262. For a full discussion of the classic distinction between sect and church, established by Ernst Troeltsch and refined by his successors in the study of religions' development, see Benton Johnson, "On Church and Sect," *Sociology of Religion, Anthology*, Knudten, pp. 123-35.
14. Weber, *Sociology of Religion*, pp. 60-61.
15. Hoffer, *True Believer*, pp. 130, 132.
16. Williston Walker, *A History of the Christian Church*, rev. (New York: Charles Scribner's Sons, 1959), p. 151.
17. St. Augustine, "The City of God," 20:9. *Great Books*, vol. 18 (Chicago: William Benton, 1952), p. 539; cf. O. E. Evans, "Kingdom of God," pp. 17-26, who sees the phrases Kingdom of God and Kingdom of Heaven as synonomous, even listing them so in the title of his article.
18. Walker, *History of Christian Church*, p. 124.
19. Wells, *Social Instututions*, pp. 262-63.
20. Weber, *Sociology of Religion*, p. 1. In the Roman Catholic Church this dispensation takes place via the Sacraments.
21. Hoffer, *True Believer*, p. 135.
22. Quoted in Walker, *History of Christian Church*, p. 262.
23. The medieval synthesis is that unity of culture, thought, and life sustained by the Roman Catholic Church, which embraced the social, economic, political, religious, and military aspects of life at the height of the Middle Ages.

CHAPTER 6. STAGE FIVE: IDENTITY

1. Loren Eiseley, *The Firmament of Time* (New York: Atheneum, 1960), pp. 13-15.
2. *Ibid.*, pp. 10-26. Catastrophism, according to Eiseley, explains, with a certain Old Testament grandeur, such things as glacial boulders scattered far from their point of origin: They were left there in some great deluge like the Noachian Flood.
3. *Ibid.*, p. 180.
4. Albert Einstein, *Out of My Later Years* (New York: Philosophical Library, 1950), p. 45.
5. Loren Eiseley, *The Man Who Saw Through Time* (New York: Charles Scribner's Sons, 1961), p. 53.
6. Benedict de Spinoza, *The Chief Works* (London: George Bell & Sons, 1883), pp. 81-119.
7. Will Durant, *The Story of Philosphy* (New York: Time-Life Books, 1962), p. 175.
8. Voltaire, as quoted in Durant, *Ibid.*, pp. 192, 225.
9. Durant, *Ibid.*, pp. 256-59.
10. Lewis White Beck, *Six Secular Philosphers* (New York: The Free Press, 1966), pp. 88-89.

NOTES FOR PAGES 60–73

11. Richard M. Brace, *The Making of the Modern World* (New York: Rinehart & Co., 1955), p. 39.
12. Erik H. Erikson, "Reflections on the Dissent of Contemporary Youth," *International Journal of Psycho-Analysis*, vol. 51 (1970), p. 13.
13. John P. Dolan, *The Essential Erasmus* (New York: New American Library, 1964).
14. William Blake, "The Everlasting Gospel."
15. Friedrich D. E. Schleiermacher, *On Religion: Speeches to Its Cultured Despisers*.
16. *Ibid*.
17. *Ibid*.
18. Ernest Renan, *The Future of Science*.
19. Paul Tillich, *Systematic Theology*, vol. 1.
20. Dietrich Bonhoeffer, *Last Letters from a Nazi Prison*.
21. Thomas J. J. Altizer, *The Gospel of Christian Atheism* (Philadelphia: The Westminster Press, 1966), p. 103.

CHAPTER 7. STAGE SIX: INTIMACY

1. Emil Brunner, *Eternal Hope* (Philadelphia: The Westminster Press, 1954), pp. 125-27.
2. Thomas Robert Malthus, *First Essay on Population* (London: Macmillan and Co., 1966), p. 14.
3. Paul R. Ehrlich, *The Population Bomb*, rev. ed. (New York: Ballantine Books, 1971), pp. 4, 15.
4. *1974 World Population Estimates* (Washington, D.C.: The Environmental Fund, 1974).
5. Ehrlich, *Population Bomb*, p. 4.
6. *Ibid.*, pp. 7-12.
7. *Special Report: Questioning the Source* (Washington, D.C.: The Environmental Fund, May 1976).
8. Donella H. Meadows, *et al.*, *The Limits to Growth*, 2nd rev. ed. (New York: New American Library, 1972), pp. 57-58.
9. *Ibid.*, p. 75.
10. *Ibid.*, pp. 78-80.
11. *Ibid.*, p. 92. It should be noted that The Club of Rome group has significantly modified its position from that of urging "no growth" to an encouragment of "selective growth," with emphasis upon voluntary actions worldwide to speed up the development of the poorer countries. *Time* (April 26, 1976), p. 56.
12. Robert L. Heilbroner, *An Inquiry into the Human Prospect* (New York: W. W. Norton & Co., 1974), pp. 63-69.
13. *Ibid.*, pp. 71-75.
14. *Ibid.*, pp. 99-104.
15. *Ibid.*, pp. 106-10.
16. Note the previous reference, Erikson, "Reflections," footnote 13, ch. 6.
17. Heilbroner, *Inquiry*, p. 115.
18. Anthony Kenny, *Wittgenstein* (Cambridge: Harvard University Press, 1973), p. 14.
19. *Ibid.*, p. 163. Wittgenstein finally settled on the language-game image partly because there is no characteristic common to every game; yet it conveys family–likeness as well as the idea of a complicated network of similarities and relationships criss-crossing and overlapping.

NOTES FOR PAGES 74-92

20. "Ms." by Gloria Maxson, copyright 1976 Christian Century Foundation. Reprinted by permission, from the April 14, 1976 issue of *The Christian Century*.
21. Casey Miller and Kate Swift, "Women and the Language of Religion," *The Christian Century* (April 14, 1976), p. 353.
22. Rita Gross, "The Image of God as Woman" (lecture, Stephens College, January 29, 1976).
23. E. Glenn Hinson, "The Problems of Devotion in the Space Age," *Review and Expositor*, vol. 71 (Summer 1974), p. 301.
24. *Ibid.*
25. Norman Pittenger, "The Incarnation in Process Theology," *Review and Expositor*, vol. 71 (Winter 1974), pp. 43-57.

CHAPTER 8. STAGE SEVEN: GENERATIVITY

1. Karl Barth, *The Word of God and the Word of Man* (New York: Harper & Row, 1957), pp. 68-69.
2. Gleason, *Growing*, pp. 105-16.
3. Julian Huxley, "Introduction," *The Phenomenon of Man*, Pierre Teilhard de Chardin. 2nd ed., rev. (New York: Harper Torchbooks, 1965), pp. 21-28.
4. Teilhard, *Phenomenon*, pp. 244-45. The advance of all together can be done under the influence of a few—but an elite few.
5. *Ibid.*, pp. 260, 262.
6. *Ibid.*, pp. 276-85.
7. *Ibid.*, p. 276.
8. Joseph Campbell, *The Masks of God: Creative Mythology* (New York: Viking Press, 1970), pp. 609-24.
9. Arthur C. Clarke, *2001: A Space Odyssey* (New York: New American Library, 1968).
10. *Ibid.*, p. 217.

CHAPTER 9. STAGE EIGHT: INTEGRITY

1. Gleason, *Growing*, pp. 117-29.
2. Jean-Paul Sartre, *No Exit*, from *The Philosophy of Jean-Paul Sartre*, ed. Robert Denoon Cumming; trans. Stuart Gilbert (New York: Random House, 1965), pp. 185-87. © 1946 by Stuart Gilbert. Used with the permission of Alfred A. Knopf, Inc.
3. Nevil Shute, *On The Beach* (New York: William Morrow & Co., 1957), p. 201.
4. *Ibid.*, p. 309.
5. There are a few intriguing parallels between *2001: A Space Odyssey* and *On The Beach*. The names of both heroes, David Bowman and Peter Holmes, have the same number of letters as does the name "Jesus Christ." Both voyages central to the respective plots trace the path of a radio signal to its source. The first source proves to be initiated by an intelligence always mysteriously in the background, but clearly interested in the fulfillment of human potential, to the point of intervention at critical historical moments to expedite the fulfillment process. In sharp contrast, the second source turns out to be a cruel chance joke of mere circumstance. And whereas the human pioneer is able to grow out of and beyond his "skin," the human victims die, prisoners of theirs.

CHAPTER 10. THE PSYCHOLOGY OF RELIGION

1. For a more thorough discussion of the philosophical roots of the psychology of religion, see G. Stephens Spinks, *Psychology and Religion* (Boston: Beacon Press, 1963), ch. 2.
2. For a more thorough discussion of Freudian psychology, see Calvin S. Hall, *A Primer of Freudian Psychology* (New York: New American Library, Mentor Books, 1954).
3. James Bissett Pratt, "The Psychology of Religion," *The Psychology of Religion*, ed. Orlo Strunk, Jr. (Nashville: Abingdon Press, 1971), p. 13.
4. Russell Olt, *An Approach to the Psychology of Religion* (Boston: Christopher Publishing, 1956), ch. 11.
5. Pratt, "Psychology of Religion," p. 15.
6. Pryns Hopkins, "A Critical Survey of the Psychology of Religion," *Psychology of Religion*, Strunk.
7. Seward Hiltner, "The Psychological Understanding of Religion," *Psychology of Religion*, Strunk.
8. Anton T. Boisen, *Out of the Depths* (New York: Harper & Brothers, 1960).
9. *Ibid.*
10. Edward E. Thornton, *Professional Education for Ministry* (Nashville: Abingdon Press, 1970), p. 70.
11. Peter Homans, *Theology After Freud* (New York: Bobbs-Merrill, 1970), pp. 94-113.
12. *Ibid.*, p. 15.
13. John B. Watson, *Behaviorism* (Chicago: University of Chicago Press, 1924), pp. 1-19.
14. Homans, *Theology After Freud*, p. 107.

CHAPTER 11. THE FOUR FUNCTIONS OF THE MIND

1. Paul W. Pruyser, *A Dynamic Psychology of Religion* (New York: Harper & Row, 1968).
2. Wayne E. Oates, *The Psychology of Religion* (Waco, Tex.: Word Books, 1973).
3. Norman Winski, *Understanding Jung* (Los Angeles: Sherbourne Press, 1971), pp. 18, 19, 24.
4. deLaszlo, *Writings of Jung*, p. 268.
5. *Ibid.*, pp. 251-53.
6. *Ibid.*, pp. 280-81.
7. Winski, *Understanding Jung*, p. 79.
8. deLaszlo, *Writings of Jung*, p. 262.
9. *Ibid.*, pp. 262-63.
10. Winski, *Understanding Jung*, pp. 72-73.
11. deLaszlo, *Writings of Jung*, p. 238.
12. Carl G. Jung, *Modern Man in Search of a Soul* (New York: Harcourt, Brace, Jovanovich, A Harvest Book, 1966), p. 93.

CHAPTER 12. SENSATION

1. Michael Malone, *Psychetypes* (New York: Pocket Books, 1977), pp. 160-88.
2. Pruyser, *Dynamic Psychology*, p. 176.

3. *Ibid.*, pp. 21-22.
4. Paul Tillich, *Dynamics of Faith* (New York: Harper & Row, Colophon Books, 1958), pp. 1, 52.
5. The World A, B, C, and D imagery was introduced and defined (although World D was only implied) in William E. Baldridge and John J. Gleason, Jr., "A Theological Framework for Pastoral Care," *The Journal of Pastoral Care*, vol. 32 (December 1978), pp. 232-38.
6. Tillich, *Dynamics*, pp. 51-52.

CHAPTER 13. FEELING

1. Malone, *Psychetypes*, pp. 131-59.
2. Carroll A. Wise, *The Meaning of Pastoral Care* (New York: Harper & Row, 1966), p. 8.
3. John T. McNeill, *A History of the Cure of Souls* (New York: Harper & Row, 1977), pp. 1-66.
4. E. Glenn Hinson, "A Brief History of Glossolalia," *Glossolalia*, Frank Stagg (Nashville and New York: Abingdon Press, 1967), pp. 71-72.
5. Wayne E. Oates, "A Socio-Psychological Study of Glossolalia," *Glossolalia*, Stagg, pp. 79, 83.
6. Tillich, *Dynamics*, p. 53.
7. *Ibid.*

CHAPTER 14. THINKING

1. Malone, *Psychetypes*, p. 102.
2. *Ibid.*, p. 130.
3. William E. Hordern, *A Layman's Guide to Protestant Theology*, rev. ed. (New York: The Macmillan Co., 1968), p. xvii.
4. *Ibid.*, p. xiv.
5. Tillich, *Dynamics*, p. 50.
6. *Ibid.*, pp. 41-43.
7. *Ibid.*, p. 101.

CHAPTER 15. INTUITION

1. Malone, *Psychetypes*, p. 194.
2. *Ibid.*, p. 216.
3. Gordon W. Allport, *The Individual and His Religion* (New York: The Macmillan Co., 1960), pp. 64-83.
4. C. Daniel Batson, "Religion as Prosocial: Agent or Double Agent?" *Journal for the Scientific Study of Religion*, vol. 15 (March 1976), pp. 31-32.
5. *Ibid.*, p. 32.
6. *Ibid.*, p. 41.
7. deLaszlo, *Writings of Jung*, p. 263.
8. Joseph Campbell, *The Hero With a Thousand Faces* (Princeton: Princeton University Press, 1972), p. 30.
9. *Ibid.*, p. 217.

CHAPTER 16. A CHRISTOLOGICAL SURVEY

1. This statement assumes a certain inertia or resistance regarding the changes required for passage from World to World, visualized in the diagram shown on page 190.

NOTES FOR PAGES 134–141

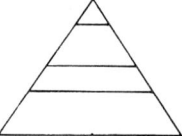

Smallest number of persons

Greatest number of persons

World D (Intuition)

World C (Thinking)
World B (Feeling)

World A (Sensation)

2. The key word here is *representative*. For example, the so-called theologies of liberation (black, female, third-world, red, *et al.*) are *not* treated in this study, on the grounds that their essence and intent originated in the social gospel movement, which *is* touched upon.
3. Karl Barth, *Church Dogmatics*, vol. 1:2 (Edinburgh: T. & T. Clark, 1956), p. 125.
4. James Leo Garrett, Jr., "A Reappraisal of Chalcedon," *Review and Expositor*, vol. 71, (Winter 1974), p. 36.
5. *Ibid.*, pp. 40-41.
6. *Ibid.*, p. 41.
7. Lonnie D. Kliever and John H. Hayes, *Radical Christianity* (Anderson, S.C.: Droke House, 1968), p. 179.
8. Walter Rauschenbusch, *A Theology for the Social Gospel* (New York: Abingdon, 1945), p. 150.
9. Kliever and Hayes, *Radical Christianity*, p. 180.
10. Barth, *Dogmatics*, vol. 4:1, pp. 126-27.
11. Hellmut Gollwitzer, *Karl Barth, Church Dogmatics, A Selection* (New York: Harper Torchbooks, 1962), p. 92.
12. Barth, *Dogmatics*, vol. 4:1, p. 136.
13. Paul Tillich, *Systematic Theology*, vol. 2. (London: James Nisbet & Co., 1957), pp. 139-41.
14. *Ibid.*, pp. 136-37.
15. Victor Lowe, "Whitehead's Metaphysical System," *Process Philosophy and Christian Thought*, ed. Delwin Brown *et al.* (Indianapolis: Bobbs-Merrill, 1971), pp. 4-20.
16. Bernard E. Meland, "The New Creation," *Process Theology*, ed. Ewert H. Cousins (New York: Newman Press, 1971), pp. 191-202.
17. Pierre Teilhard de Chardin, "My Universe," *Process Theology*, Cousins, pp. 249-55.
18. W. Norman Pittenger, *The Word Incarnate* (New York: Harper & Row, 1959), p. 188.
19. Wolfhart Pannenberg, *Jesus-God and Man* (Philadelphia: The Westminster Press, 1968), p. 212, 53.
20. E. Frank Tupper, "The Christology of Wolfhart Pannenberg," *Review and Expositor*, vol. 71 (Winter 1974), p. 65.
21. Pannenberg, *Jesus-God*, p. 98.
22. Wolfhart Pannenberg, *Basic Questions in Theology*, vol. I (Philadelphia: Fortress Press, 1971), p. xvi.
23. Altizer, *The Gospel of Christian Atheism*.
24. Harvey Cox, *The Feast of Fools* (Cambridge: Harvard University Press, 1969), p. 139.
25. *Ibid.*, p. 141.

CHAPTER 17. A CHRISTOLOGICAL CRITIQUE

1. Tillich, *Systematic Theology*, vol. 2, p. 12.
2. John A. T. Robinson, *Honest to God and the Debate* (London: SCM Press, 1963), pp. 11-18.

CHAPTER 18. A CHRISTOLOGICAL PRESCRIPTION

1. Leszek Kolakowski, "The Priest and the Jester."
2. Kurt Vonnegut, *Slapstick* (New York: Delacorte Press, 1976), pp. 184-85.
3. *Ibid.*, pp. 185-86.

CHAPTER 19. PRESCRIPTION APPLIED TO WORLD C

1. E.g., see Mary Daly, *Beyond God the Father* (Boston: Beacon Press, 1973), pp. 13-43.
2. E.g., see Albert Schlitzer, ed., *The Spirit and Power of Christian Secularity* (Notre Dame, Ind.: University of Notre Dame Press, 1969), p. 102.
3. Teilhard, *Phenomenon*, pp. 261-62.
4. Brown et al., *Process Philosophy and Christian Thought*, pp. 13, 32.
5. Teilhard, *Phenomenon*, p. 250.
6. Alfred North Whitehead, *Process and Reality* (New York: The Free Press, 1969), p. 307.
7. Arthur Berndtson, "A Theory of Radical Creativity," *The Modern Schoolman*, vol. 53 (November 1975), pp. 9, 3, 15.
8. George Gamow, *One Two Three . . . Infinity* (New York: Bantam Books, 1971), p. 231.
9. Teilhard, *Phenomenon*, pp. 65, 144-46.
10. Steven Rose, *The Conscious Brain* (New York: Random House, Vintage Books, 1976), pp. 34, 181.
11. Daniel Day Williams, "God and Man," *Process Theology*, Cousins, p. 186.
12. Berndtson, "Theory of Radical Creativity," pp. 4, 5.
13. Hordern, *Layman's Guide*, p. 61.
14. Teilhard, *Phenomenon*, pp. 262-63.
15. Kurt Vonnegut, Jr., *Cat's Cradle* (New York: Dell Publishing, 1970), p. 118. Copyright © 1963 by Kurt Vonnegut, Jr. Reprinted by permission of Delacourt Press/Seymore Lawrence.
16. *Ibid.*, p. 90.
17. *Ibid.*, pp. 14, 177, Dedication.
18. *Ibid.*, pp. 11, 53, 67.

CHAPTER 20. PRESCRIPTION APPLIED TO WORLD B

1. Faber's image of the hospital chaplain as clown (Heije Faber, *Pastoral Care in the Modern Hospital* [Philadelphia: The Westminster Press, 1971]) and Switzer's extrapolation of that image to ministry at large (David K. Switzer, "The Minister as Pastor and Person," *Pastoral Psychology*, vol. 24 [Fall 1975], pp. 52-64) are fascinating precursors to harlequinesque pastoral care, although no sustained attempt is made by either to backtrack the analogy to its source in Christology.
2. McNeill, *Cure of Souls*, pp. 87, 324.
3. Baldridge and Gleason, "Theological Framework."
4. *Ibid.*

5. *Ibid.*
6. Thanks to William E. Baldridge for building upon the association between Worlds A and D and arriving at the conclusion that generalizations about the exercise of pastoral authority should be the same for both worlds.
7. Marshall Kilduff and Ron Javers, *The Suicide Cult* (New York: Bantam Books, 1978).

CHAPTER 21. PRESCRIPTION APPLIED TO WORLD A

1. Karl W. Deutsch, *Nationalism and Its Alternatives* (New York: Alfred A. Knopf, 1969), pp. 3, 6, 4-20.
2. Arthur Hertzberg, ed., *Judaism* (New York: George Braziller, 1962), p. 11.
3. Norman J. Faramelli, "Ecological Responsibility and Economic Justice," Andover Newton *Quarterly*, vol. 11 (November 1970), pp. 81-93.
4. Alvin Toffler, *Future Shock* (New York: Bantam Books, 1971), p. 478.
5. Charles A. Reich, *The Greening of America* (New York: Random House, 1970), p. 307.
6. Paul R. Ehrlich, *How To Be A Survivor* (New York: Ballantine Books, 1971), p. 64.
7. *Time* (April 26, 1976), p. 56.
8. John B. Cobb, Jr. (address delivered to 1978 Annual Conference Association for Clinical Pastoral Education, Inc., Seattle, November 10, 1978).
9. The college town is Columbia, Missouri. At this time, participating organizations include the Assault, Abuse, and Rape Crisis Center; members of the Central Missouri Pastoral Care Association—in Columbia: Bethel Baptist Church, Calvary Baptist Church, First Baptist Church, Memorial Baptist Church, Columbia United Church of Christ, Broadway Christian Church, First Christian Church, Calvary Episcopal Church, St. Andrew's Lutheran Church, Trinity Lutheran Church, First Presbyterian Church, Trinity Presbyterian Church, Community United Methodist Church, Missouri United Methodist Church, and Wilkes Boulevard United Methodist Church—and in Jefferson City: the Catholic Diocese, Community Christian Church, First Christian Church, and First Presbyterian Church; also, Boone County Hospital; Columbia Manor Care Center; Columbia Police Department; Columbia Regional Hospital; Columbia Visiting Nurses Association; Ellis-Fischel State Cancer Hospital; Everyday People; Lenoir Memorial Home; Mid-Missouri Mental Health Center; and University of Missouri Medical Center.

EPILOGUE

1. Samuel Southard (lecture on Abraham Kaplan, *The Conduct of Inquiry* [San Francisco: Chandler Publishing, 1964], Central State Hospital, Milledgeville, Ga., October 1968).